basic FORTRAN IV with WATFOR and WATFIV

Self-Instructional Manual and Text

CHARLES R. BAUER, B.S., M.ED.
Adjunct Assistant Professor
Computer Science Department
Illinois Institute of Technology
Chicago
Assistant Principal in charge of Scheduling
Lane Technical High School
Chicago

ANTHONY P. PELUSO, B.S., M.S.
Associate Professor
Wilbur Wright College
Mathematics Department

ADDISON-WESLEY PUBLISHING COMPANY
Reading, Massachusetts · Menlo Park, California · London · Don Mills, Ontario

Reproduced by Addison-Wesley from camera-ready copy prepared by the authors.

 Printed in the United States of America. Published simultaneously in Canada. Library of Congress Catalog Card No. 74-135.

ISBN 0-201-00411-9
ABCDEFGHIJ-AL-7987654

CONTENTS

SECTION ONE

CHAPTER ONE	INTRODUCTION TO COMPUTERS	3
	Steps in Problem Solving	6
	Using Self-Instructional Materials	9
CHAPTER TWO	FUNDAMENTALS OF THE FORTRAN LANGUAGE	11
	The FORTRAN Character Set	11
	The Assignment Statement	14
	Identifiers and Arithmetic Expressions	14
	Exponentiation	21
	Order of Operations	27
	Parentheses	32
	Assignment Statements in Sequence	40
	Modes	49
	Conversion of Modes	57
CHAPTER THREE	INPUT/OUTPUT	67
	The PRINT Statement	68
	The STOP Statement	72
	The END Statement	72
	The READ Statement	74
CHAPTER FOUR	BRANCHING	83
	Statement Numbers	85
	The GO TO Statement	87
	The IF Statement	90
	Sample Program	96
CHAPTER FIVE	LOOPING	103
	The DO Statement	103
	The CONTINUE Statement	106
CHAPTER SIX	PROGRAM ASSEMBLY AND SAMPLE PROGRAMS	121
	Analyzing the Problem	121
	Flow Charting	122
	Coding	124
	The Hollerith Card	126
	Deck Assembly	130
	Sample Program One	132
	Sample Program Two	135
	Partial Programs	138

SECTION TWO

CHAPTER SEVEN	INPUT/OUTPUT WITH FORMAT	145
	FORMAT Free Input/Output	145
	The FORMAT Statement	145
	READ and PRINT with FORMAT	146
	The Output FORMAT Statement	147
	The Input FORMAT Statement	153
	Preparing Data Cards	155
	F Specifications	163
	I Specifications	165
	X Specifications	167
	H Specifications	169
	E Specifications	171
	A Specifications	174
	DATA Statements	176
	Multiple Record Formats	177
	Carriage Control	178
	General READ and WRITE Statements	179
	Continuation Cards	179
	Type Declarations	180
	Comment Cards	182
CHAPTER EIGHT	ARRAYS AND THE DIMENSION STATEMENT	183
	Array Notation	183
	Input for an Array	185
	Operations on Elements of an Array	187
	Sum of the Elements of an Array	187
	Output for an Array	188
	The DIMENSION Statement	188
	Arrays with More Than One Subscript	194
	Variations in the Use of Arrays	196
CHAPTER NINE	LOGICAL CONTROL	199
	Simple GO TO	199
	Computed GO TO	200
	Assigned GO TO	203
	Arithmetic IF	204
	Logical IF	207
CHAPTER TEN	ITERATIVE TECHNIQUES	213
	Nested DO Loops	217
CHAPTER ELEVEN	SUBPROGRAMS	223
	Library Functions	223
	Arithmetic Statement Function	228
	FUNCTION Subprogram	230
	SUBROUTINE Subprogram	232

SECTION THREE

APPENDIX I	PRACTICE PROBLEMS	239
APPENDIX II	HINTS TO PRACTICE PROBLEMS	247
APPENDIX III	SAMPLE PROGRAMS THREE TO TEN	253
APPENDIX IV	SOLUTIONS TO PARTIAL PROGRAMS	279
APPENDIX V	ANSWERS TO TESTS	287

PREFACE

This book is intended to serve primarily as a self-instruction text for the student who wishes to familiarize himself with the fundamentals of computer programming. It is written for the beginner who has little or no knowledge of computers or computer programming. The ability to read at a high school level and a knowledge of mathematics up to and including first-year high school algebra is all the preparation needed.

This text presents the essentials of the computer language FORTRAN IV along with WATFOR and WATFIV. The name FORTRAN is derived from FORmula TRANslation. WATFOR (a derivative of FORTRAN) is so named because it was developed at the University of Waterloo (WATerloo FORtran). FORTRAN was originally designed for writing computer programs that would solve scientific and engineering problems involving mathematical computations. WATFOR was developed to provide this capability to large numbers of students which requires faster processing of programs to handle the larger volume of users. WATFIV comes from WATerloo Fortran IV.

This text has been designed to provide the essential information required for the reader to learn, as quickly as possible, to write computer programs in FORTRAN using the WATFOR or WATFIV compilers. At appropriate points, exercises are presented. Self-tests will be found at the end of Chapters Two, Three, Four, and Five. Answers to all exercises and solutions to the tests are provided.

Section Three includes a series of Practice Problems to aid the reader in gaining proficiency in writing programs. Hints to writing these programs are also offered, and to further aid the reader a set of Sample Programs are presented in Appendix III.

Since FORTRAN, like other programming languages suffers from many versions, an attempt has been made to caution the reader at points where differences can be expected due to variations in the language. When problems arise that can be attributed to a language variation the best approach is to consult the specific manual which describes the operating system and the particular version of FORTRAN available.

The authors are indebted to the following individuals for their assistance in preparing the manuscript.

Sandra Flemming

Robrick Granhold

Barry Rosen

Laurel Spitzbarth

C.R.B.

A.P.P.

SECTION ONE

CHAPTER ONE

INTRODUCTION TO COMPUTERS

The reader is well aware of the tremendous problem-solving powers of the computer. Man is constantly attempting to solve problems, and the computer has now become an additional tool to aid him. Before beginning the study of a computer language, it will be helpful to have at least a fundamental understanding of the similarities between problem solving by humans and problem solving by machines. Most problems presented to us as humans involve: (1) some information, upon which (2) some action is required, to obtain (3) results. For convenience, let us call phase (1) <u>input</u>, phase (2) <u>manipulation</u>, and phase (3) <u>output</u>.

To solve most problems, we must be capable of reading and understanding the input, performing the manipulation required, and producing the output.

Computers operate in much this same fashion. They must accept input, perform manipulation, and produce output. However, inside a computer no intelligence is present to guide these processes. Instead, the computer must depend on a complete, detailed set of directions which precisely describes how each step of each phase of the problem solution is to be performed. These directions, called a computer program, reside in the memory of a computer.

The primary component of a computer is a large information storage device, suggestively called a memory. The most common basic building block of a computer memory is a tiny iron-ferrite donut-shaped object called a magnetic core. The electronic characteristics of a core are such that it may be circularly magnetized in one of two directions, viz. ⊚ or ⊚ .

The electronic circuitry of a memory is able to (1) force the magnetization of a core to be in one direction or the other; (2) find out the direction of magnetization. Thus, any core may exist in one of two possible states (directions of magnetization), which may be set or interrogated.

These two states (different directions of magnetization) may be given names such as on and off, yes and no, 1 and 0, etc. If these states are considered to be 1 and 0, we will be able to see how it is possible for a computer to store a number.

We begin by recalling the idea of place value in our familiar decimal system.

A number such as 345 in decimal notation should be thought of as

1000	100	10	1	→ place value
	3	4	5	→ number

that is, $345 = 3 \times 100 + 4 \times 10 + 5 \times 1$.

Recalling that only ones and zeros are available in the computer, we assign our place value as follows:

8	4	2	1 → place value
	1	0	0 → number

that is, $4 = 1 \times 4 + 0 \times 2 + 0 \times 1$. A five would be represented as 101; that is, $5 = 1 \times 4 + 0 \times 2 + 1 \times 1$.

The following table indicates both the decimal representation and the computer representation of the integers from zero to nine.

Decimal Representation		Computer Representation			
		8	4	2	1
0		0	0	0	0
1		0	0	0	1
2		0	0	1	0
3		0	0	1	1
4		0	1	0	0
5		0	1	0	1
6		0	1	1	0
7		0	1	1	1
8		1	0	0	0
9		1	0	0	1

In summary, by assigning to a given set of only four core positions the appropriate place values, as described above, and by assigning either 1 or 0 to the two possible states of each core, any integer from 0 to 9 can be conveniently represented in the computer.

In a very similar manner, letters of the alphabet, punctuation symbols, and steps of a computer program may be stored in a computer memory. This is accomplished by assigning a specific code, consisting of several 0's and 1's, to each quantity to be represented.

The specific information required to encode the FORTRAN language will be provided after the reader is familiar with the fundamentals of the language. This coding will not require the use of 0's and 1's; the examples on the preceding page are only to indicate how symbols can be represented inside a computer. FORTRAN coding uses letters, numbers, and familiar symbols.

STEPS IN PROBLEM SOLVING

In order to solve a given problem through the use of a digital computer, it is necessary to (1) understand and analyze the problem, (2) outline the solution, (3) create a step by step set of instructions for the computer, and (4) prepare these instructions in a form acceptable to the computer.

A convenient method of outlining the solution to a problem is by creating a flow chart. A flow chart is made up of a combination of geometric symbols which represent the various functions required in the solution of the problem. These symbols are connected with lines and arrows, which indicate the logical flow of problem solution.

Flow charts are used extensively in solving problems involving computers. However, the central idea of a written sequence of steps to be performed may apply to any problem-solving situation. Before a person solves any problem, some planning should be done. For very simple problems, often the planning is done unconsciously. For some problems involving several actions (such as baking a pie), perhaps a list of the steps will suffice, but for more complex situations, the necessary directions may require consideration of the possibility that a certain step cannot be done, and that something else must be tried before continuing. In other words, alternatives must be considered. This latter situation is best represented by a flow chart.

The illustration on the next page shows how one might use a flow chart to describe the various steps involved in obtaining a soft drink from a vending machine.

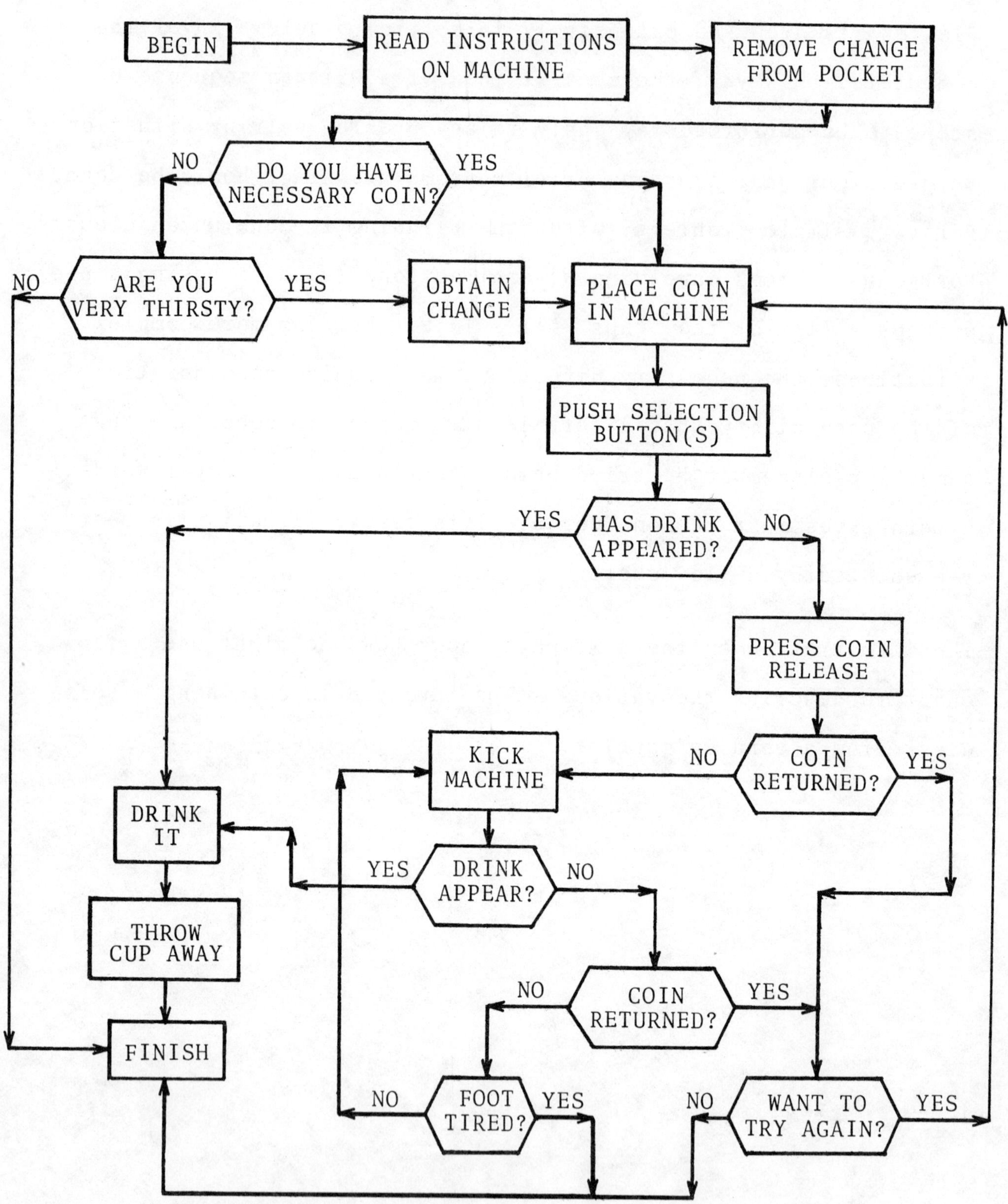

FLOW CHART: OBTAINING A DRINK

The flow chart in the illustration may appear to involve some unnecessary effort to solve such a simple problem, but the intention is to demonstrate that the steps of a process can be organized through the use of a flow chart, and to suggest that this method can be applied to more complex situations.

The symbols used for flow charting in FORTRAN, and the application of flow chart techniques to computer problem situations will be discussed as the reader becomes familiar with the FORTRAN language. Similarly, the writing of step by step instructions (coding), and preparation of these instructions in a form acceptable to the computer will be taken up at a later time.

USING SELF-INSTRUCTIONAL MATERIALS

The self-instruction portion of this text is presented in two forms. First, the reader will find paragraphs of written exposition which vary in length from a few lines to several lines. Second, the reader will find small units of information or short questions called frames. Each frame is numbered and requires an active response in the form of a word, symbol, or phrase. The points at which a response is required are indicated by a dotted line across the page.

As you study this material follow these steps:

1) Place a shield over the page so that only the first frame is exposed down to the dotted line;
2) Read the information carefully to the point at which a response is required;
3) After deciding on the proper response, write it on an auxiliary response sheet;
4) Slide the shield down to uncover the correct response, and any additional remarks accompanying it;
5) Verify your response. If it is correct, continue with the next frame. If it is incorrect, reread the frame with the correct response in mind;
6) When turning pages, avoid looking at any responses on the new page by covering the page with the shield as soon as possible;
7) Do all exercises and chapter tests as they are encountered.

Sample frame:

1.01 In this text the reader is made aware that a response is required by the appearance of a _____ _____ across the page.

\- -

dotted line

CHAPTER TWO

FUNDAMENTALS OF THE FORTRAN LANGUAGE

THE FORTRAN CHARACTER SET

The character set used in FORTRAN consists of:

a) Alphabetic Characters

Capital letters of the English alphabet, from A through Z

b) Numeric Characters

First ten numerals, from 0 through 9

c) Special Characters

= + - * / ( ) , . $ '

d) Blank Character

Combinations (one or more) of the above characters have unique meanings to the FORTRAN language. These combinations (called symbols) are of various types such as

a) Combinations of alphabetic characters, which form words, either built-in (Key Words) or Identifiers (programmer chosen words).

b) Combinations of numeric characters, which form numbers.

c) Combinations of special characters which form:

1) Arithmetic Operators

Addition	Subtraction	Multiplication
+	-	*
Division	**Assignment**	**Exponentiation**
/	=	**

2) Grouping Characters

Comma	Parentheses	Apostrophe
,	( )	'

Other combinations will be defined as we study the language.

2.01 In the FORTRAN language, the capital letters of the English alphabet from _____ through _____ are used.

- -

A Z

2.02 FORTRAN also uses the first ten numerals from _____ through _____.

- -

0 9

2.03 The parentheses, comma, and apostrophe are all used in FORTRAN. (True or False)

- -

True

2.04 The period is used in FORTRAN. (True or False)

- -

True

2.05 The symbols # ; : are used in FORTRAN. (True or False)

- -

False

2.06 The Blank Character is a legal FORTRAN character. (True or False)

- -

True

2.07 FORTRAN makes use of the same symbols for addition and subtraction that are used in ordinary arithmetic. The symbol for addition in FORTRAN is _____ and the symbol for subtraction is _____.

- -

+ -

2.08 In FORTRAN, the symbol used to designate multiplication is * (asterisk). A*B would mean that A is to be _____ by B.

- -

multiplied

2.09 In FORTRAN, the symbol used to designate division is / (slash). An expression such as A/B would mean that A is to be _____ by B.

- -

divided

THE ASSIGNMENT STATEMENT

A computer programming language such as FORTRAN, like any language, has a vocabulary and rules of grammar and punctuation. When you have learned the rules and vocabulary of FORTRAN, you will then be ready to program the computer. To write a program for the computer, the programmer constructs a sequence of statements which indicate to the computer the specific steps to be performed in solving the problem.

The most basic statement in FORTRAN is the Assignment statement. It is used whenever the programmer requires the computer to perform arithmetic calculations. Statements such as

```
W=X+Y+Z
AREA=SIDE*SIDE
```

are examples of Assignment statements.

The statement W=X+Y+Z instructs the computer to find the sum of X, Y, and Z and assign the value to W. Of course, the computer must in some way be informed of the values of X, Y, and Z.

The statement AREA=SIDE*SIDE instructs the computer to multiply the value of SIDE times SIDE, obtain the result, and then assign this value to AREA.

IDENTIFIERS AND ARITHMETIC EXPRESSIONS

In these examples, W, X, Y, Z, AREA, and SIDE are called Identifiers. Identifiers are words (or single letters) which the programmer invents to represent the quantities involved in his problem.

Notice that the programmer may choose entire words as Identifiers to represent quantities; however, various versions of the FORTRAN language have different restrictions concerning the length of Identifiers. The first character of an Identifier must be a letter and the other characters must be either letters or digits. None of the special characters, including the blank, may be used in an Identifier. Identifiers should not, in general, exceed six characters in length.

Listed below are examples of words which can or cannot be used as Identifiers.

Legal Identifiers	Illegal Identifiers
A	1A (first character must be alphabetic)
AREA	AR.CIR (special character not permitted)
A1	AR EA (blank not permitted within an Identifier)
XNUM	
SANDY	
KARON	
AREA1	
XINT	
A1B2	
A12345	

2.10 In the FORTRAN language, the computer can easily be instructed to perform the basic operations of addition, subtraction, multiplication, and division.

The Assignment statement W=X+Y+Z instructs the computer to perform the operation of _____.

- -

addition

2.11 The sum of X, Y, and Z can be computed and the result assigned to W by the statement W=X+Y+Z.

When the Assignment statement W=X+Y+Z is executed by the computer, the result is assigned to the Identifier called _____.

- -

W

2.12 In a similar manner, the Assignment statement can be used to instruct the computer to perform the operations of subtraction, multiplication, and division.

The statement AREA=SIDE*SIDE instructs the computer to perform the operation of _____ and to assign the result to an Identifier called _____.

- -

multiplication AREA

2.13 The basic arithmetic operations are indicated in FORTRAN by the symbols

addition	+	subtraction	-
division	/	multiplication	*

The expression A-B indicates that the computer is to perform the operation of _____.

- -

subtraction

2.14 The expression A/B indicates that the computer is to perform the operation of _____.

- -

division

2.15 The expression A+B-C indicates that the computer is to _____ the values of A and B, and then _____ the value of C from the result.

- -

add subtract

2.16 The expression A*X+B instructs the computer to perform the operations of _____ and _____.

- -

multiplication addition

2.17 The FORTRAN expression A*B/C indicates that the value of _____ is to be _____ by the value of B and the result is to be divided by the value of _____.

- -

A multiplied C

2.18 If the programmer wishes to instruct the computer to subtract the value of B from the value of A, the correct expression would be _____.

- -

A-B

2.19 In an Arithmetic expression, two arithmetic operation symbols must not appear adjacent to each other. A*-B is a legal FORTRAN expression. (True or False)

- -

False

Every Assignment statement has a left side and a right side. The right side may consist of any legal FORTRAN expression. The left side must be a legal Identifier. After the right side is evaluated, assignment must be made to an Identifier on the left of the assignment symbol; therefore, statements such as

```
A+B=C
```

are illegal in the FORTRAN language.

EXERCISE 2.01 EXPRESSIONS AND ASSIGNMENT STATEMENTS

Write the following expressions in FORTRAN notation. Use capital letters for Identifiers.

a) a+b+c ____________

b) x+y-z ____________

c) $\frac{a}{b} + \frac{c}{d}$ ____________

d) ax+by+cz ____________

Write the following formulas as FORTRAN Assignment statements. Use capital letters for Identifiers.

e) x=prt ____________

f) w=x+y+z ____________

g) A=bh ____________

h) Area equals height times base ____________

See the following page.

Solutions to EXERCISE 2.01 EXPRESSIONS AND ASSIGNMENT STATEMENTS

a) A+B+C

b) X+Y-Z

c) A/B+C/D

d) A*X+B*Y+C*Z

e) X=P*R*T

f) W=X+Y+Z

g) A=B*H

h) AREA=HEIGHT*BASE

Note: In d, e, g, and h the FORTRAN multiplication symbol * must appear.

EXPONENTIATION

If you understand the Assignment statement, you are now capable of instructing the computer to perform the arithmetic operations of addition, subtraction, multiplication, and division.

Another basic operation that the computer can perform is exponentiation. Exponentiation refers to the raising of a quantity to a designated power (squaring, cubing, etc.).

Examples:

3^2 (in arithmetic) means 3 is to be multiplied by itself.

Therefore,

$3^2 = 3\times3=9$ (the process is called squaring)

In the above example, the 3 would be called the base and the 2 would be called the exponent.

The quantity which is raised to the indicated power is the base. The indicated power is the exponent.

$4^3 = 4\times4\times4=64$ (the process is called cubing)

$2^3 = 2\times2\times2=8$

$1.5^2 = 1.5\times1.5=2.25$

2.20 If the number 2 is raised to the 4th power, 2^4, the result is _____.

- -

16 $2^4 = 2\times2\times2\times2=16$

2.21 3^4 = _____.

- -

81 $3^4 = 3\times3\times3\times3=81$

Exponents are not limited to integral values. It is sometimes necessary to raise a quantity to a fractional power.

$25^{.5} = 25^{1/2} = \sqrt{25} = 5$ (the .5 power indicates the square root)

$16^{.25} = 16^{1/4} = \sqrt[4]{16} = 2$ (the .25 power indicates the fourth root)

$4^{1.5} = 4^{3/2} = \sqrt{4^3} = \sqrt{64} = 8$

2.22 If the number 9 is raised to the .5 power, the result is _____.

- -

3 $9^{.5} = 9^{1/2} = \sqrt{9} = 3$

2.23 If the number 81 is raised to the .25 power, the result is _____.

- -

3 $81^{.25} = 81^{1/4} = \sqrt[4]{81} = 3$

2.24 When 4 is raised to the 2.5 power, the result is _____.

- -

32 $4^{2.5} = 4^{5/2} = \sqrt{4^5} = \sqrt{1024} = 32$

2.25 In FORTRAN, the symbol used to designate exponentiation is ** (double asterisk). For example, if we want to raise the quantity 2 to the fourth power, in FORTRAN we would write:

2**4

The operation sign ** (double asterisk) tells the computer to raise a quantity to the indicated _____.

- -

power

2.26 In the FORTRAN expression K**7, the value of _____ would be raised to the _____ power.

- -

K 7th

2.27 The FORTRAN language allows much more complex expressions in working with exponentiation than the previous examples indicate. For example, the base need not be an integer value.

In FORTRAN, the expression 2.5**2 would have the value _____.

- -

6.25

2.28 Similarly, the exponent need not be an integer. The statement, X=A**.5 is a valid statement.

If we want to raise A to the .25 power, we would write _____.

- -

A**.25

Note: In FORTRAN both the base and the exponent may be legal FORTRAN expressions.

In this chapter we have discussed both expressions and Assignment statements. It is very important that you understand the difference between these two important ideas. The expressions used in the examples simply indicate arithmetic calculations to be performed. An expression, as used here, would not constitute a legal statement in FORTRAN. The Assignment statement also performs arithmetic calculations, but in addition, because of the symbol = and the Identifier on the left, the result of the calculation is stored as the value of the Identifier on the left. The Assignment statement is the most fundamental statement in the FORTRAN language.

2.29 Construct an Assignment statement which instructs the computer to raise the quantity N to the ninth power, and assign the answer to the Identifier RESULT.

- -

```
RESULT=N**9
```

2.30 In arithmetic, the formula for the area of a square is given by $A=S^2$. How would you translate this formula into a FORTRAN Assignment statement?

- -

```
A=S**2      A=S*S      AREA=SIDE**2      AREA=SIDE*SIDE
```

are all correct solutions

EXERCISE 2.02 EXPONENTIATION

Write the following expressions in FORTRAN notation, and perform the calculations:

		FORTRAN	Result
a)	2^3	2**3	8
b)	3^3		
c)	10^2		
d)	5^3		
e)	2^5		
f)	10^4		
g)	2.5^2		
h)	$625^{.5}$		
i)	$25^{1.5}$		
j)	$16^{.25}$		

See the following page.

Solutions to EXERCISE 2.02 EXPONENTIATION

a)	2**3	8
b)	3**3	27
c)	10**2	100
d)	5**3	125
e)	2**5	32
f)	10**4	10000
g)	2.5**2	6.25
h)	625**.5	25
i)	25**1.5	125
j)	16**.25	2

ORDER OF OPERATIONS

Note: Readers familiar with "order of operations" from mathematics should not make unwarranted assumptions at this point.

A single expression may require several operations to be performed. For example, the expression

```
A**2+B*3.2-C
```

involves the operations of exponentiation, multiplication, addition, and subtraction. One can easily imagine much more complicated expressions than the one indicated in the example. The computer can easily and quickly calculate very complicated expressions; however, the computer can perform only one operation at a time. For this reason, the computer will perform the operations in a specific order and, of course, the programmer must be aware of this order.

In any FORTRAN expression not containing parentheses all operations of exponentiation (if any are present) will be performed first. Next, any operations of multiplication and/or division will be performed, and last, any operations of addition and/or subtraction.

This rule must be strictly observed if the desired results are to be obtained.

In summary, the FORTRAN hierarchy is as follows:

1) All exponentiation
2) All multiplication and/or division (from left to right)
3) All addition and/or subtraction (from left to right)

2.31 In FORTRAN, the value of the expression

2+2*2

would be _____.

- -

6 since multiplication is performed before addition

2+2*2

2+4

6

2.32 Multiplication and division are at the same level of hierarchy. They are performed in the order indicated from left to right.

In FORTRAN, the expression A/B*C would be evaluated by first performing the operation of _____ and then the operation of _____.

- -

division multiplication

2.33 In algebra, A/B/C would be ambiguous; in FORTRAN, it means _____ divided by _____ and the quotient divided by _____.

- -

A B C

2.34 In the FORTRAN expression, A**2+B*3.2-C the operation of _____ would be done first, then the operation of _____, and last, the operations of _____ and _____.

- -

exponentiation multiplication addition subtraction

2.35 Assume that for the FORTRAN Assignment statement,

X=A**2+B*3.2-C

the computer has been previously given the following values of A, B, and C: A=4.0, B=5.0, and C=6.0, what value would be assigned to the Identifier X?

- -

26.0

```
A**2+B*3.2-C
4.0**2+5.0*3.2-6.0
16.0+5.0*3.2-6.0
16.0+16.0-6.0
32.0-6.0
26.0
```

2.36 Given the FORTRAN statement,

X=W/Y+Z

indicate which of the two following statements it represents:

a) $x = \frac{w}{y} + z$ b) $x = \frac{w}{y + z}$

- -

a

Note: The correct FORTRAN expression for example b would require the use of parentheses. It would be X=W/(Y+Z). This will be discussed in the section on parentheses.

EXERCISE 2.03 ORDER OF OPERATIONS

In each of the expressions below indicate which two quantities are involved in the first operation to be performed:

a) X+Y-Z ____X and Y____

b) A*B+C**2 ________

c) JOHN+JOE/JIM ________

d) MARY+JOAN+LETTY*JUNE ________

e) X+Y-B**2.5+R*3.1 ________

In the following FORTRAN Assignment statements assume that the Identifier RADIUS has the value 5.0

```
DIAM=2.0*RADIUS
CIRCUM=2.0*3.14*RADIUS
AREA=3.14*RADIUS**2
```

Determine the value which will be assigned to the Identifier,

f) DIAM ________

g) CIRCUM ________

h) AREA ________

See the following page.

Solutions to EXERCISE 2.03   ORDER OF OPERATIONS

a) X and Y

b) C and 2

c) JOE and JIM

d) LETTY and JUNE

e) B and 2.5

f) 10.0

g) 31.4

h) 78.5

PARENTHESES

In the preceding sections, you have learned how to instruct the computer to perform simple arithmetic operations. In this section, you will learn how to make use of parentheses, as symbols of grouping, so that you will have greater flexibility in constructing expressions and Assignment statements. The necessity for parentheses, or at least some symbol to designate the grouping of quantities, is easily seen by the following example:

Suppose that we would like to find the sum of A and B and then double the result. A suitable expression is required in order to indicate that A is to be added to B and the result is to be multiplied by 2.0. Notice also, that in this case, we require that the normal order of operations be altered. A FORTRAN expression that will satisfy all of these requirements is

```
2.0*(A+B)
```

When the computer encounters quantities enclosed in parentheses, the computation required within the parentheses will be performed before any other operations are begun.

2.37 When an expression such as

$$\frac{w}{y + z}$$

is encountered in mathematics, w is to be divided by the sum of y and z. To express this in FORTRAN notation, we would write it as _____.

- -

W/(Y+Z)

2.38 In the FORTRAN expression, A+B/C+D the first operation to be performed would be ____.

- -

division

2.39 In the FORTRAN expression, (A+B)/(C+D) the first operation to be performed would be ____.

- -

addition

Note: The computation is performed inside the parentheses first.

2.40 Assume that the computer has been given previously the following values: I=10, J=4, K=2, L=5, and then encounters the Assignment statement, M=(I+J)/(K+L).

What value will be assigned to Identifier M?

- -

2 (I+J)/(K+L)
(10+4)/(2+5)
14/7
2

2.41 Within parentheses, the normal order of operations will be followed until all computations are performed. In the expression, A*(B**2+C) the first operation to be performed will be _____, the second operation will be _____, and the last operation will be _____.

- -

exponentiation addition multiplication

Note: All computations will be done inside the parentheses according to the order of operations.

2.42 Parentheses may be used even though they are not required. The expression X*Y+W*Z would be the same as (X*Y)+(W*Z). The expression A/B+C/D would be equivalent to _____.

- -

(A/B)+(C/D)

2.43 Each use of a left parenthesis requires the use of a right parenthesis, and vice versa. The expression (A+(4.1*A) is invalid because of the missing _____ parenthesis, or because of the extra _____ parenthesis.

- -

right left

2.44 Write the expression $\frac{a}{bc}$ in FORTRAN notation.

- -

A/(B*C) the parentheses are necessary

As you have seen, parentheses represent a very convenient symbol for grouping quantities, and can also be very useful when you wish to alter the normal order in which operations are performed. Expressions and formulas expressed in conventional notation can easily be changed to FORTRAN notation. Some examples of situations in which parentheses are necessary are listed below.

Conventional notation	FORTRAN notation
$\frac{x}{a + b}$	X/(A+B)
u^{n-2}	U**(N-2)
$s = \frac{a}{x - y}$	S = A/(X-Y)
$s = \frac{rs - a}{r - s}$	S = (R*S-A)/(R-S)

2.45 A pair of parentheses may be completely contained within another pair. These are called nested parentheses. When the computer encounters this situation, it simply performs the computation in the innermost parentheses first.

In the expression, ((X*Y+B)-S)/R the expression contained in the innermost parentheses is _____.

- -

X*Y+B

2.46 In the expression, ((X*Y+B)-S)/R the first operation to be performed will be _____, and the second operation will be _____.

- -

multiplication addition

2.47 In the expression given in 2.46, the next operation will be _____, and the last operation will be _____.

- -

subtraction division

2.48 The computer will first completely evaluate the expression in the innermost parentheses and then use that value in computing the quantities in the next outer parentheses.

When parentheses are nested, computation begins in the _____ parentheses.

- -

innermost

A summary of the rules concerning parentheses follows:

1) Parentheses are used to group quantities;
2) Parentheses can be used to alter the normal order of operations;
3) A parenthesized expression must be evaluated before any other operations are performed;
4) The normal order of operations prevails within each pair of parentheses;
5) The result obtained within any pair of parentheses is used in the overall expression;
6) When parentheses are nested, computing begins in the innermost pair;
7) Every left parenthesis must be balanced with a right parenthesis, and vice versa.

Note: An effective practice to observe when working with parentheses is to use them whenever any doubt is present. Additional parentheses, even though not required, will do no harm to a FORTRAN statement; however, if parentheses are missing when they are required, the results may be incorrect.

EXERCISE 2.04   PARENTHESES

In each of the FORTRAN Assignment statements below, indicate the operation that will be performed first:

a) Y=A+X**2+(X*Y) ____________________

b) Z=M/N+(J*K)+M+N ____________________

c) FAHR=X+Y*(W/Z) ____________________

d) TEMP=((X+Y)*Z+G) ____________________

e) T=B*G**3+(Y+G) ____________________

See the following page.

Solutions to EXERCISE 2.04 PARENTHESES

a) Multiplication

b) Multiplication

c) Division

d) Addition

e) Addition

ASSIGNMENT STATEMENTS IN SEQUENCE

In several preceding examples, we have indicated that the computer must be informed of the values contained in an expression before the expression can be evaluated. We will now demonstrate one way in which this can be done. A statement such as

```
X=5.1+2.2
```

is a valid Assignment statement in FORTRAN. When this statement is encountered, the computer will add 5.1 to 2.2, obtain 7.3 as the result, and assign the value 7.3 to X. If the Identifier X appears in a succeeding Assignment statement (to the right of the assignment symbol), the computer will automatically supply 7.3 as the value of X.

Example:

If the computer encounters the following two Assignment statements in sequence:

```
X=5.1+2.2
A=X+10.0
```

7.3 will be assigned to X, and when A=X+10.0 is executed, the computer will supply 7.3 as the value for X, add 7.3 to 10.0, and assign the value 17.3 to A.

As you can see from the preceding example, the Assignment statement is a very powerful statement. It performs calculations and stores the result, which is then available on demand.

As you might expect, we may have several Assignment statements in sequence.

Example:

```
X=4.1+2.2
Y=2.3+3.4
Z=4.1+0.0
W=X+Y+Z
```

When all four of these statements have been executed, the value of W will be the sum of 6.3 + 5.7 + 4.1, which is 16.1, and the value 16.1 will be assigned to W.

As you can see from the preceding example, Z = 4.1 + 0.0 is a valid FORTRAN Assignment statement. It should not be surprising to learn that statements such as

```
A=5.1
FIRST=7.75
RADIUS=15.2
```

are also valid Assignment statements in FORTRAN.

Note, however, that in every example of an Assignment statement there is only one Identifier on the left side of the assignment symbol, and no operational signs appear on the left side of the assignment symbol.

The entire preceding discussion indicates only one way in which we may inform the computer of the values contained in an expression, so that the expression may be evaluated. This method, although completely workable, has certain limitations in programming, and a more powerful method will be presented later.

2.49 An Assignment statement need not have any Identifiers on the right side of the assignment symbol.

The Assignment statement X=5.1+6.2 is valid in FORTRAN. (True or False)

- -

True

2.50 Only one Identifier is permitted to the left of the assignment symbol in an Assignment statement.

The Assignment statement X+Y=Z is a valid FORTRAN statement. (True or False)

- -

False

2.51 No operational signs are permitted to the left of the assignment symbol in an Assignment statement.

The Assignment statement X**2=X*X is a valid FORTRAN statement. (True or False)

- -

False

2.52 The computer encounters the following two statements in FORTRAN:

```
A=6.1
X=7.0*A
```

After both statements have been executed, the value assigned to X will be _____.

- -

42.7

2.53 After the statements

```
A=5.2
B=3.4
X=A+B
```

have been executed in FORTRAN, the value assigned to X will be _____.

- -

8.6

2.54 In FORTRAN, after the statements:

```
BASE = 6.0
ALT = 5.3
AREA = BASE*ALT
```

have been executed, the value assigned to AREA will be _____.

- -

31.8

Every Assignment statement is executed in two distinct stages. In the first stage, the computation is performed on the right of the assignment symbol. In the second stage, the computed value is assigned to the Identifier on the left of the assignment symbol. The same Identifier may appear several times in a sequence of statements and may also appear on both the left and right side of the assignment symbol in a particular statement.

Example:

```
I=5
.....
.....
I=I+1
```

When the computer encounters the above statements, first the value 5 is assigned to I. Then, since I also appears on the right side of a later Assignment statement, the value of 5 is supplied for I, and 1 is added to 5. The result, 6, is then assigned to I, and the previous value of I is lost. This example demonstrates that the Identifier on the left side of an Assignment statement may have a different value from the same Identifier on the right side of the statement.

Statements in sequence, such as

```
I=5
.....
.....
I=I+1
```

occur very frequently in computer programs. Their significance and use will be discussed in a later section.

2.55 In FORTRAN, a statement such as J=J+1 is a legal statement. (True or False)

- -

True

2.56 In FORTRAN, the latest value of an Identifier is called the current value of the Identifier.

After executing the following sequence of statements, what is the current value of B?

```
A=5.2
B=A+3.3
B=B+2.4
```

- -

10.9

2.57 If the following sequence of statements appeared in a FORTRAN program, what would be the current value of W?

```
A=5.0
B=6.0
C=A+B
D=A*C
E=D-C
W=A+B+C+D+E
```

- -

121.0

Statements are executed, by the computer, in the order in which they appear. The following example indicates the importance of ordering statements correctly.

Case 1	Case 2
DEPTH=5.2	DEPTH=5.2
WIDTH=3.1	WIDTH=3.1
HEIGHT=10.3	HEIGHT=10.3
AREA=DEPTH*WIDTH	VOLUME=AREA*HEIGHT
VOLUME=AREA*HEIGHT	AREA=DEPTH*WIDTH

Note: In Case 1, after all statements have been executed, VOLUME will have the value 166.036. In Case 2, when the computer attempts to evaluate VOLUME=AREA*HEIGHT, AREA will not yet have been defined, and the computer will be unable to evaluate AREA*HEIGHT.

EXERCISE 2.05 ASSIGNMENT STATEMENTS IN SEQUENCE

Consider the following sequence of Assignment statements to be part of a computer program. The statements are to be executed in the order in which they are written. After each statement has been executed, indicate the current values of each of the Identifiers A, B, and C. Assume initial values of A=0.0, B=0.0, and C=0.0

	A	B	C
a) A=7.5+B+C	7.5	0.0	0.0
b) B=A+5.5	____	____	____
c) C=B+10.5	____	____	____
d) A=A-2.5	____	____	____
e) B=B+C	____	____	____
f) C=A+B	____	____	____
g) C=B/A+3.3	____	____	____
h) A=A*A	____	____	____
i) B=A*C	____	____	____

See the following page.

Solutions to EXERCISE 2.05 ASSIGNMENT STATEMENTS IN SEQUENCE

	A	B	C
a)	7.5	0.0	0.0
b)	7.5	13.0	0.0
c)	7.5	13.0	23.5
d)	5.0	13.0	23.5
e)	5.0	36.5	23.5
f)	5.0	36.5	41.5
g)	5.0	36.5	10.6
h)	25.0	36.5	10.6
i)	25.0	265.0	10.6

MODES

A beginning FORTRAN programmer should understand clearly the difference between real mode and integer mode, and avoid mixing modes in the same expression. (An exception to the rule against mixing modes is discussed in Chapter Three.) In general, it is a safe rule for the beginner in the FORTRAN language that the modes should not be mixed in the same expression. The exceptions to this rule will be discussed in Chapter Three.

The programmer must direct the computer as to which mode to employ. The computer will use real mode if a decimal point appears in the constants; thus, 5.2, 100.1, and 7.0 are real. Absence of a decimal point, such as in the constants 46 or 1071, directs the computer to function in integer mode.

2.58 There are two kinds or modes of arithmetic used in FORTRAN: real and integer.

Constants are the actual numbers in expressions.

In the following statement

```
AREA=3.1416*R*R
```

the constant is _____.

- -

3.1416

2.59 Some examples of real numbers are:

3.1416 4.0 53.2 177.6

In the following statement

AREA=3.1416*R*R

the mode of the constant 3.1416 is _____.

- -

real

2.60 Some examples of integer numbers are:

8 10 214 7542

The mode of these constants is _____.

- -

integer

Identifiers are also subject to the rule against mixing modes. In order to enable the programmer to direct the computer, the letters I, J, K, L, M, and N have been reserved to indicate integer mode. All other letters direct the computer to operate in real mode.

If the Identifier consists of more than one letter, or a combination of letters and numerals, the <u>first</u> letter in the Identifier determines the mode. Thus, L, K, JOB, MASS, and NUM would be integer mode Identifiers; A, F, SUM, XMASS, and ANUM would be real mode.

2.61 All integer mode Identifiers begin with the letters I, J, K, L, M, or N.

In the following statement

```
I=M*3
```

the I, M, and 3 are all in the same mode. (True or False)

- -

True

2.62 All real mode Identifiers begin with letters other than I, J, K, L, M, or N.

A, B, C, D, L, and X are all real mode Identifiers.

(True or False)

- -

False L is an integer mode Identifier

Note: In general, the real mode is used in a computation. The integer mode is used for counting and for certain specialize but useful operations, which will be discussed in Chapter Five.

2.63 In the following example, 4.0 is assigned to the Identifier DIAM. The expression, DIAM*3.1416 instructs the computer to multiply DIAM and 3.1416 and assign the value to the Identifier CIRCUM.

```
DIAM=4.0
CIRCUM=DIAM*3.1416
```

The real mode of DIAM is established by the _____ letter.

The presence of a _____ point in 3.1416 establishes real mode for this constant.

- -

first decimal

2.64 We can use from one to six characters for a FORTRAN Identifier.

The following are all legal Identifier names:

S1234	POD	X	SQUARE
RST	XMILE	ROOT	AREA

(True or False)

- -

True

2.65 The mode is determined by the first character, which must be alphabetic.

The Identifiers in the statement

```
FORCE=XMASS*ACCEL
```

are all in _____ mode.

- -

real

2.66 All Identifiers and constants appearing on the right side of an Assignment statement must be of the same mode.

e.g. `AREA=1./2.*(B*H)`

The elements to the right of the assignment symbol comprise the expression. They must be of the same _____.

- -

mode

2.67 The expression R+1 is illegal because of mixed (or different) modes. The Identifier R is of real mode and the constant 1 is of integer mode.

This illegal expression can be corrected by writing it in real mode as _____.

- -

R+1. or R+1.0

Some exceptions to the mixed mode rule occur in exponentiation. The expression X**6, although of mixed mode, will be accepted and produce the desired result; however, the same expression written as X**6.0 would cause an error if X were negative since an exponent in real mode causes a logarithmic evaluation to take place. In addition, a base of integer mode cannot be used with an exponent of real mode.

2.68 An exponent of integer mode may be used with a base of either integer mode or real mode.

The statements

B=X**2

and

K=J**2

are both legal. (True or False)

- -

True

2.69 A real exponent can be used only with a real base.

The statements

B=X**.5

and

K=J**.5

are both legal. (True or False)

- -

False (B=J**.5 is illegal; an integer base cannot be used with a real exponent.)

EXERCISE 2.06 MODES

Each of the following Assignment statements contain a mixed mode expression. In each example make all changes necessary so that each expression will be in real mode. Change any Identifiers of integer mode to real by preceding them with an X.

a) AREA=L*W ____________________

b) C=89*D+2 ____________________

c) VOLUME=L*W*H ____________________

d) FEET=INCHES/12. ____________________

e) CENT=2.54*IN ____________________

f) HYR=K**.5 ____________________

Each of the following Assignment statements contain a mixed mode expression. In each example make all changes necessary so that each expression will be in integer mode. Change any Identifiers of real mode to integer by preceding them with an I.

g) J=J+1.0 ____________________

h) K=89*D+2 ____________________

i) IPERIM=2.*(L+W) ____________________

j) IRAD=DIAM*2 ____________________

See the following page.

Solutions to EXERCISE 2.06 MODES

a) AREA=XL*W

b) C=89.*D+2.

c) VOLUME=XL*W*H

d) FEET=XINCH/12. (XINCHES has too many characters.)

e) CENT=2.54*XIN

f) HYR=XK**.5

g) J=J+1

h) K=89*ID+2

i) IPERIM=2*(L+IW)

j) IRAD=IDIAM*2

CONVERSION OF MODES

FORTRAN rules permit quantities on opposite sides of the assignment symbol to be of different modes. This allows the programmer to change or convert values from real to integer mode and from integer mode to real mode.

e.g. real to integer / integer to real

```
real to integer          integer to real
      I=X                      XI=I
      JIM=3.75                 Y=2
      L=A+B*C                  A=I+J*K
```

When an Assignment statement involves conversion, the expression to the right of the assignment symbol is completely evaluated, and the value obtained is assigned, (in the required mode) as designated by the Identifier to the left of the assignment symbol.

Conversion from integer to real mode in a statement such as Y=2 will cause a value of 2.0 to be assigned to Y.

When assigning real values to integer Identifiers, the programmer must remember that the result will be an integer. Since a statement such as JIM=3.75 must have an integer result, the whole number portion of the value will be retained and the decimal portion will be dropped. Therefore, after the statement JIM=3.75 is executed, the integer 3 will be assigned to JIM. Notice that the number 3.75 is not "rounded off". Whenever real values are converted to integer the decimal portion is always dropped. This feature is called truncation.

2.70 Integer arithmetic produces integer results in all arithmetic operations, including division. This can cause errors.

When the statement

N=5/2

is executed, the value assigned to N is 2 because in integer division only the integer portion of the quotient is calculated.

When the statement

X=17/3

is executed the value assigned to X will be _____.

- -

5.0

2.71 Caution must be used when assigning a real number to an integer Identifier.

Consider the following Assignment statement

M=3.1416

The resulting value assigned to the Identifier M is _____.

- -

3

.72 In the following case, assume N, K, and J have the values of 11, 3, and 4 respectively.

I=N/K+J

The results of this evaluation would assign the value of _____ to the Identifier I.

- -

7

Note: 11/3 would result in a quotient of 3, due to integer division.

2.73 Expressions in real mode can be evaluated and then assigned to an integer Identifier.

Consider the following example:

Assume that X and R have values of 26.4 and 10. respectively.

J=X/R

The results of this conversion will assign a value for J of _____.

- -

2 (26.4/10. = 2.64; when the value is converted to integer, it becomes 2.)

EXERCISE 2.07 TRUNCATION

Evaluate the following Assignment statements.

	Values	Statements	Results
a)	I=5 K=4 L=2	N=I/L*K	
b)	X=4.1	N=X**2	
c)	B=2.0 X=1.998	N=X/B	
d)	N=13 J= 4	N=N/J*J-N	

See the following page.

Solutions to EXERCISE 2.07 TRUNCATION

a) 8

b) 16

c) 0

d) -1

CHAPTER TWO TEST

PART 1. True or False

____ 1) All of the capital letters of the English alphabet from A through Z are legal characters in FORTRAN.

____ 2) The numerals from 0 through 9 may be used in FORTRAN.

____ 3) To indicate addition and subtraction in FORTRAN, one uses the same symbols as in ordinary arithmetic.

____ 4) In FORTRAN, to indicate the multiplication of a times b, the correct expression would be AB.

____ 5) In FORTRAN, if we wish to express $\frac{a}{b}$, the correct expression is A/B.

____ 6) In the FORTRAN language, the value of 6**2 is 12.

____ 7) X+Y-Z is an example of an Assignment statement in FORTRAN.

____ 8) A programmer may invent words to represent the quantities in his problem.

____ 9) In FORTRAN, generally, an Identifier must not contain more than six characters.

____ 10) JEFF is a legal Identifier in FORTRAN.

____ 11) 25B is a legal Identifier in FORTRAN.

____ 12) Assuming the computer has been informed of the values of B and C, upon encountering the statement A=B+C, the computer will add the values of B and C and assign the result to A.

____ 13) In FORTRAN, every Assignment statement must contain the assignment symbol.

____ 14) The most fundamental statement in the FORTRAN language is the Identifier.

____ 15) In the expression SUE+CHRIS+SANDY/RALPH, the first operation that will be performed is division.

____ 16) An expression free of exponents should contain elements which are of the same mode.

____ 17) The mode of a real value may be changed by assigning it to an integer Identifier.

____ 18) In a FORTRAN expression, multiplication is always performed before division.

____ 19) In the expression ((A*B)+5.)**7, the first operation to be performed is exponentiation.

____ 20) If only one pair of parentheses is encountered in a FORTRAN expression, the computation within the parentheses will be done before other operations are performed.

____ 21) Parentheses may be used in an expression to alter the usual order of operations.

____ 22) When parentheses are nested, calculation is begun in the innermost pair.

____ 23) In FORTRAN, every left parenthesis requires a right parenthesis.

____ 24) Within a given pair of parentheses, the normal order of operations prevails.

____ 25) Parentheses must never be used unless they are actually required.

____ 26) SUM=(RATIO*LAST-FIRST)/(RATIO-1) is a legal Assignment statement in FORTRAN.

____ 27) E/R=IA+IB+IC is a legal Assignment statement in FORTRAN

____ 28) When converting from real mode to integer mode, fractions will be truncated.

____ 29) X=J/N is a legal conversion from integer to real mode.

____ 30) In the Assignment statement, MIKE=JIM/JEFF, if the value 26 is assigned to JIM and 4 is assigned to JEFF, 6.5 will be the current value of MIKE.

PART 2. Matching

For each entry on the left, find the <u>most</u> appropriate entry on the right. Use each answer only once.

____ 1)	real Identifier	(a)	?
____ 2)	mixed mode	(b)	9
____ 3)	illegal character	(c)	A(B+C)*D)
____ 4)	grouping characters	(d)	X+Y=Z
____ 5)	assignment symbol	(e)	X/A+B
____ 6)	exponentiation	(f)	KARO
____ 7)	real constant	(g)	/
____ 8)	3*2	(h)	RON
____ 9)	addition symbol	(i)	6
____ 10)	$\frac{x}{a} + b$	(j)	A**B
____ 11)	invalid expression	(k)	( )
____ 12)	illegal statement	(l)	X/(A+B)
____ 13)	$\frac{x}{a+b}$	(m)	X=I
____ 14)	3**2	(n)	=
____ 15)	division symbol	(o)	DIST=RATE*TIME
____ 16)	Assignment statement	(p)	AREA=LENG*WIDT
____ 17)	real to integer	(q)	*
____ 18)	integer Identifier	(r)	5.5
____ 19)	multiplication symbol	(s)	+
____ 20)	integer to real	(t)	I=X

Verify your results before proceeding to the next chapter.

See Answers to Tests, Appendix V.

CHAPTER THREE

INPUT/OUTPUT

In Chapter Two you learned that FORTRAN makes it possible to express a mathematical statement by means of the Assignment statement. In Chapter Three Input/Output statements will be discussed. The programmer must be able to supply the computer with all information necessary for the execution of his program. After the necessary calculations have been performed, the results, or solutions, must be returned to the programmer in some acceptable form. The FORTRAN language I/O (Input/Output) statements allow for the transfer of data between the computer and the various Input/Output devices.

Data transmission, the process of getting information or data into the computer and returning results, is the basic function of input and output statements.

3.01 The most common forms of computer output are punched cards and printed pages. Throughout our discussions in Chapter Three, assume the output will be printed.

What form of computer output will be assumed in Chapter Three?

- -

the printed page

THE PRINT STATEMENT

The output statement PRINT allows the programmer to specify a sequence of Identifier values to be printed. A PRINT statement has the form:

PRINT, list

The word PRINT followed by a comma and a list consisting of one or more Identifiers separated by commas is a PRINT statement.

Listed below are examples of PRINT statement construction:

```
PRINT, AREA
PRINT, LENGTH, WIDTH, AREA
```

3.02 The PRINT statement in the FORTRAN language must be constructed in accordance with the rules stated above.

In this statement,

```
PRINT AREA
```

the current value of the Identifier AREA will be printed. (True or False)

- -

False There is a comma omitted between PRINT and AREA.

3.03 In the construction of PRINT statements, commas within the list must be observed. Given the statement,

```
PRINT, LENGTH WIDTH AREA
```

the computer would be incapable of printing values for the Identifiers: LENGTH, WIDTH, and AREA. (True or False)

- -

True Identifiers in the list must be separated by commas.

3.04 The PRINT statement is constructed as follows: the word PRINT followed by a comma, and a list of Identifiers separated by commas.

Construct a PRINT statement to provide output for the Identifiers SIDE and AREA.

- -

PRINT, SIDE, AREA

3.05 In the FORTRAN language, the output statement PRINT is used to exhibit the answers or solutions to a problem in the form of a printed page.

Answers to problems are transmitted back to the programmer in printed form by use of an _____ statement.

- -

output or PRINT

3.06 The PRINT statement operates as follows: the current values of the Identifiers are printed according to the order in which the Identifiers are listed in the PRINT statement.

In the FORTRAN output statement,

PRINT, LENGTH, WIDTH, HEIGHT, VOLUME

the current value of the Identifier _____ will appear first on the printed page.

- -

LENGTH

Note: The list may contain Identifiers of different modes.

If the PRINT statement in frame 3.06 were executed, four values would be printed on the output page.

Generally, unless modified by an advanced technique, one line of output, containing a value for each Identifier in the list, is produced each time a PRINT statement is executed.

3.07 Given the problem: Find the area of a square with the side equal to 5.5. One of the first instructions to the machine could be the Assignment statement,

```
SIDE=5.5
```

The statement needed to calculate the area could be _____.

- -

AREA=SIDE*SIDE or AREA=SIDE**2

3.08 Our program segment now contains two statements,

```
SIDE=5.5
AREA=SIDE*SIDE
```

Each of the above FORTRAN statements is an Assignment statement. (True or False)

- -

True

3.09 In this program segment, if we add an output statement,

```
SIDE=5.5
AREA=SIDE*SIDE
PRINT, SIDE, AREA
```

and the above segment were executed, the output page would have how many values printed on it?

- -

two

3.10 Which Identifier value will appear first on the output page?

- -

5.5 The value of the Identifier SIDE.

Note: Values as actually printed may be in the form

0.xxxxxxxE yy

This means the number .xxxxxxx times 10 raised the power yy.

e.g.

Computer notation	Meaning
0.8725000E 01	8.725
0.5725000E 00	.5725
0.4260000E 03	426.
0.3200000E-03	0.00032

Integer values will be printed as integers.

We have now discussed two types of FORTRAN statements - the Assignment statement and the PRINT statement. Using these two statements, we may direct the computer to perform certain calculations and to print the results of these calculations. For example:

```
SIDE=5.5
AREA=SIDE*SIDE
PRINT, SIDE, AREA
```

will direct the computer to calculate the area of the square whose side equals 5.5 and to print the values for SIDE and AREA. However, for us to complete even a simple FORTRAN program, we have need for two additional statements - the STOP and the END.

THE STOP STATEMENT

The STOP statement consists of the word STOP. It signifies the logical termination of the program and directs the computer to cease processing the program.

THE END STATEMENT

The END statement consisting solely of the word END informs the computer that the program has been read into the computer and directs the computer to begin processing the program. The END statement must be the last statement in the program.

We have now considered the statements needed to write a complete program.

```
SIDE=5.5
AREA=SIDE*SIDE
PRINT, SIDE, AREA
STOP
END
```

3.11 The four FORTRAN statements discussed thus far are _____, _____, _____, and _____.

- -

Assignment, PRINT, STOP, END

3.12 In the program presented above how many Identifier values will be printed?

- -

two

3.13 In the example discussed above, we called for the values of two Identifiers in the PRINT statement.

If nine Identifiers are listed in the PRINT statement, how many output values will be printed?

- -

nine

3.14 Many simple problems can be solved and the programs written using Assignment, PRINT, STOP and END statements. As an example, if we wished to find the volume of a box with dimensions 3.5 by 4.1 by 6.3, one program solution might be

```
WIDTH=3.5
XLENG=4.1
HEIGHT=6.3
VOLUME=WIDTH*XLENG*HEIGHT
PRINT, WIDTH, XLENG, HEIGHT, VOLUME
STOP
END
```

How many Identifier values will be printed on the output page?

- -

four

THE READ STATEMENT

The input statement READ, allows the programmer to assign values to Identifiers by reading new values. The READ statement has the form

```
READ, list
```

The word READ followed by a comma and a list consisting of one or more Identifiers separated by commas is a READ statement.

Listed below are examples of READ statement construction.

```
READ, RADIUS
READ, HOURS, RATE, TAX
READ, A, B, C, ROOT1, ROOT2
```

The following sequence of FORTRAN statements,

```
SIDE=5.5
AREA=SIDE*SIDE
PRINT, SIDE, AREA
STOP
END
```

is an example of a complete FORTRAN program. This program is extremely limited because it can be used only to calculate the area of one square. In this section, a more powerful method of supplying input values to the computer will be discussed.

3.15 In the above example, the value of SIDE was assigned with the statement,

```
SIDE=5.5
```

If we replace this with the statement,

```
READ, SIDE
```

a value or number is read from a list of values following the program, and is assigned to the Identifier SIDE each time the READ statement is executed.

The list of values to be read into the computer with a READ statement is called a data list.

Programs using READ statements are very flexible, since Identifiers can be assigned different values each time the READ statement is executed.

PRINT is the FORTRAN statement used for output, READ is the statement used for _____.

- -

input

Note: The input statement READ allows the programmer to assign values to Identifiers by inputting new values.

3.16 A list containing values to be read into the computer by a READ statement is called a data list. The data contained in the data list are separated by commas or one or more blanks.

Which group, 1 or 2, consisting of a READ and its corresponding data list, is correct?

```
1 [ READ, LENGTH, WIDTH
    84, 39.1248

2 [ READ, ABLE, DOG, CAT
    2, 4.3
```

- -

1 (In 2, only two values are present, and the READ statement has three Identifiers.)

Note: The data list does not follow the READ statement. The placement of the data list in the program will be discussed in a later section.

3.17 Write a READ statement to assign two values read from a data list to the Identifiers XLNGTH and WIDTH.

- -

READ, XLNGTH, WIDTH

3.18 How would the data to be read by the READ statement in frame 3.17 appear in order to assign XLNGTH a value of 400.17, and WIDTH a value of 200.08?

- -

400.17, 200.08

or

400.17 200.08

This illustration shows the logic in thinking necessary to compute the area of a square. This program will process a single case or card.

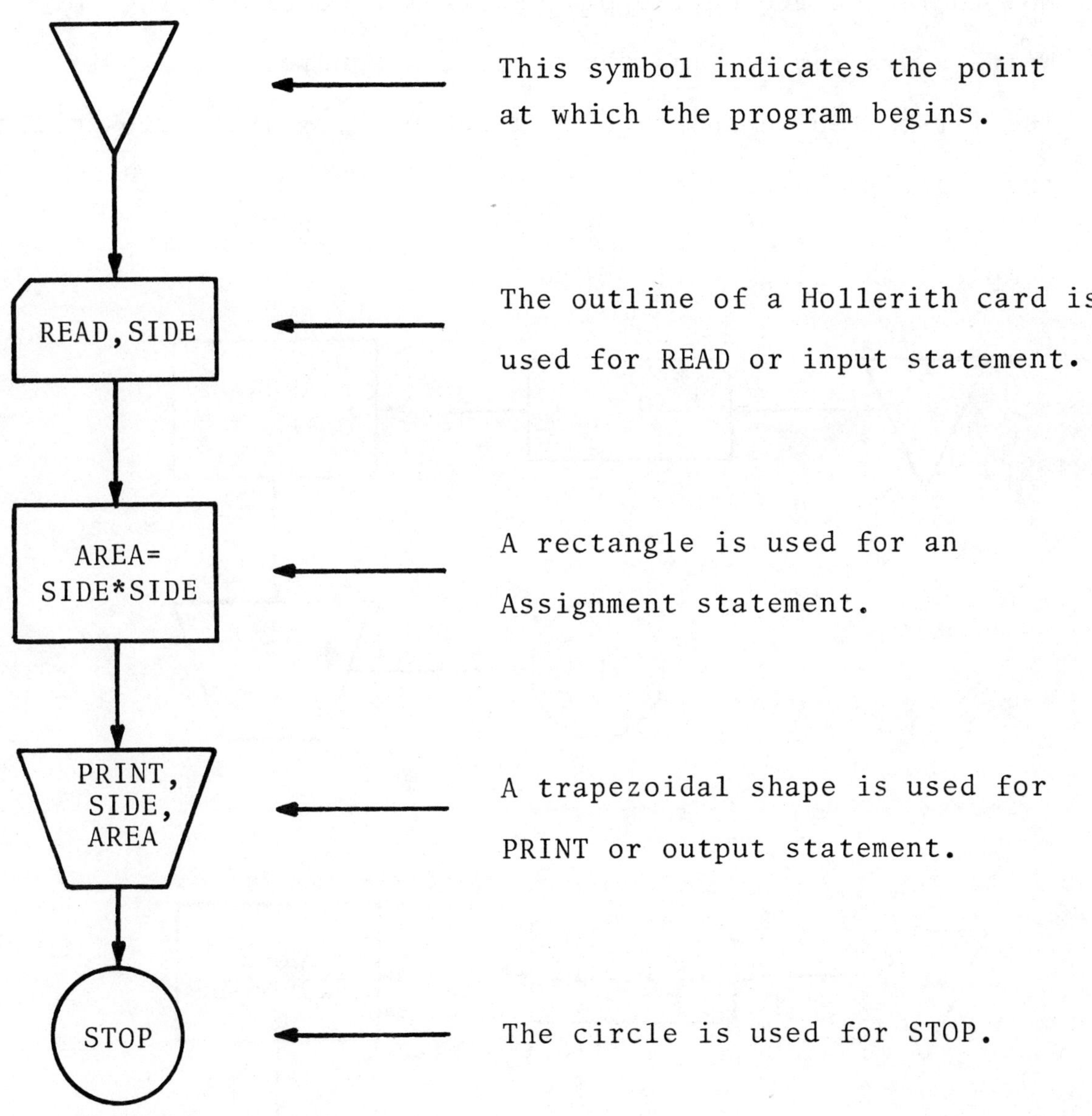

READ,SIDE
AREA=
SIDE*SIDE
PRINT,
SIDE,
AREA
STOP
This symbol indicates the point
at which the program begins.
The outline of a Hollerith card is
used for READ or input statement.
A rectangle is used for an
Assignment statement.
A trapezoidal shape is used for
PRINT or output statement.
The circle is used for STOP.

3.19 Our list of FORTRAN statements now totals five. What are they?

- -

Assignment PRINT STOP END READ

3.20 Now to review the entire process from problem to program: Write a program to find the area of a square.

The first step in approaching a new problem is to flow chart the logic.

Complete the flow chart below:

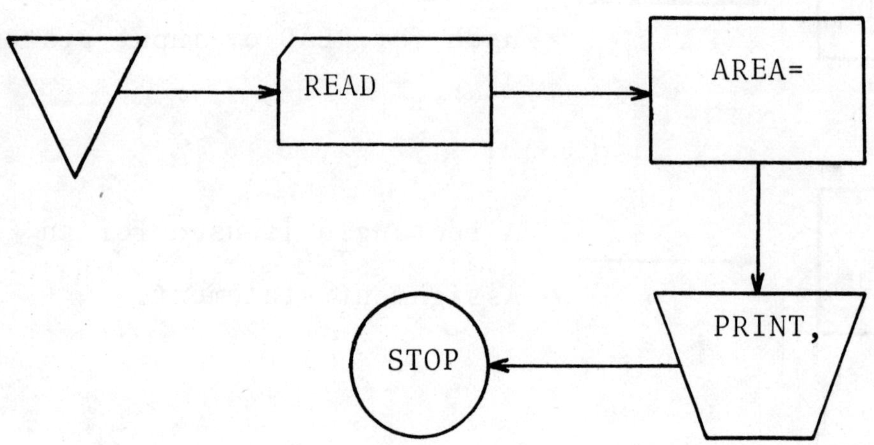

- -

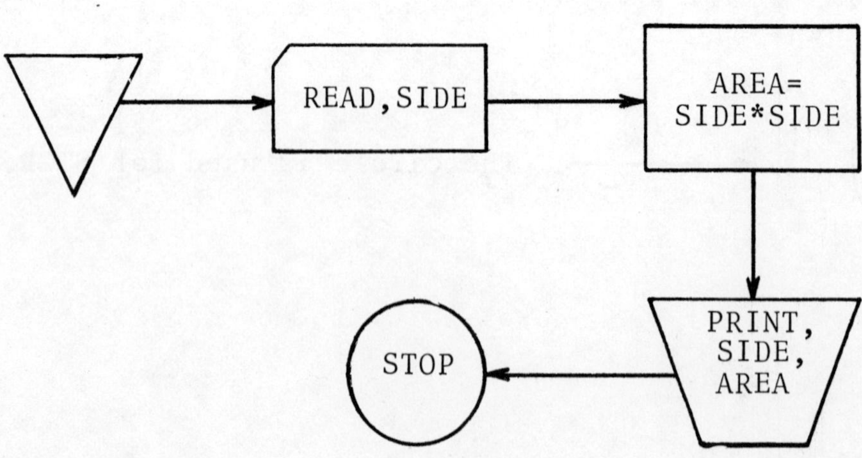

3.21 After we have constructed the flow chart, the next step is coding (the writing of the sequences of statements based on the flow chart).

Code the flow chart in frame 3.20.

- -

```
READ,SIDE
AREA=SIDE*SIDE
PRINT,SIDE,AREA
STOP
END
```

3.22 The computer is capable of reading data at the time of program execution. The READ statement contains a list of Identifiers, the values of which are read from the data list each time the READ statement is executed. The statement,

```
READ,LENGTH,WIDTH,HEIGHT
```

causes the computer to read how many values from the data list?

- -

three

3.23 The PRINT statement causes values to be displayed to the programmer. The statement,

```
PRINT,ABLE,ZOO
```

will cause the computer to write how many values on the output page?

- -

two

CHAPTER THREE TEST

PART 1. Given the problem: Write a program to find the area of a circle. Use RADIUS and AREA as Identifiers. Use the formula

$$A = 3.14R^2$$

a) Complete the flow chart below:

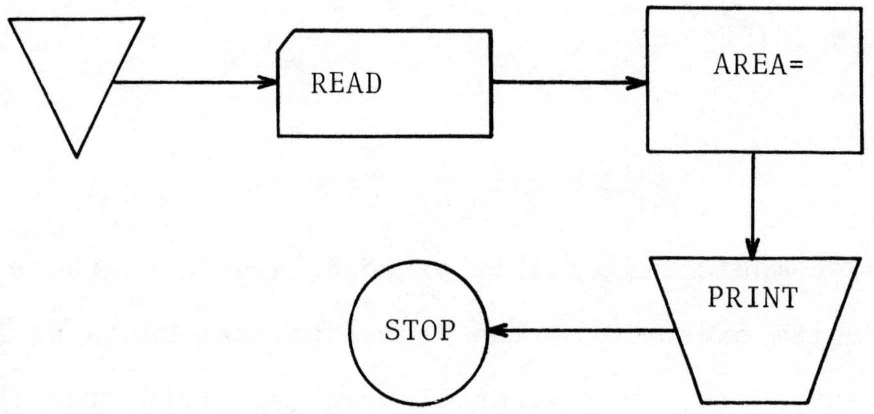

b) Code the flow chart in part a.

PART 2. Given the program:

```
READ,XL,W,H
V=XL*W*H
PRINT,XL,W,H,V
STOP
END
```

Do the following matching exercise:

_____	1) Identifier	a)	READ,XL,W,H
_____	2) Input statement	b)	PRINT,XL,W,H,V
_____	3) Assignment statement	c)	XL
_____	4) Output statement	d)	V=XL*W*H

PART 3. Find and correct any errors in the following FORTRAN statements:

a) READ UP DOWN a) ______________________________

b) PRINT,A B C b) ______________________________

c) a=2.4 c) ______________________________

d) STOP d) ______________________________

e) A+B=C e) ______________________________

f) PRINT HEIGHT,WIDTH, f) ______________________________

g) READ AT,OUCH,BOG g) ______________________________

Verify your results before proceeding the next chapter.

See Answers to Tests, Appendix V.

CHAPTER FOUR

BRANCHING

The most sophisticated program discussed in Chapter Three was able to process only a few data values. Common sense indicates that a programmer faced with the problem of computing the area of one square or finding the volume of one box could calculate the answer by hand much more rapidly than he could produce the computer program necessary to do the job. The value of a computer lies in its ability to rapidly repeat a series of operations as many times as is necessary. This can be accomplished in FORTRAN by the use of a control statement which creates an unconditional branch.

Since the use of an unconditional branching statement may cause the computer to repeat a set of instructions indefinitely, an additional control statement called a conditional branching statement will often be required.

The use of both conditional and unconditional branching statements will be presented in this chapter.

4.01 FORTRAN statements are normally executed by the computer in the order in which they are presented to the computer. The statements,

```
AREA=XLENG*WIDTH
VOLUME=AREA*HEIGHT
```

would be executed in the order presented. Should the order of the above statements be interchanged? (Yes or No)

- -

No (because the value of AREA should be available in order to execute the statement VOLUME=AREA*HEIGHT correctly)

4.02 The next series of frames will be used to introduce the use of control statements with which the programmer can alter the normal order of execution of statements.

In order to alter the normal execution of statements, control statements may be used. (True or False)

- -

True

4.03 A control statement is a statement which may cause the computer to execute statements in an order other than the normal sequential order.

A control statement changes the _____ in which statements are executed.

- -

order

STATEMENT NUMBERS

When statements are to be executed in a fashion other than sequential, there must be some way to identify or refer to the statement which is to be executed next, but is not next in sequence. Statements are identified by assigning numbers to them.

4.04 Particular FORTRAN statements may be referenced if they have a _____ _____ to identify them.

- -

statement number

In FORTRAN programs, any statement may be assigned a number; however, no two statements may be assigned the same number in any one program. The statement number is assigned arbitrarily and placed to the left of the statement to which it is assigned.

4.05 In FORTRAN, any statement may be prefixed by a statement number. This statement number is an arbitrarily chosen integer placed to the left of the statement.

e.g.

```
427  A=B*C
```

The FORTRAN statement above has a statement number of _____.

- -

427

4.06 Any statement may have a statement number, but no two statements may have the same statement number.

The FORTRAN statement,

```
11  TAX=AMOUNT*RATE
```

is correct. (True or False)

- -

True

4.07 Statement numbers may be used with any statement but a statement number should be used only where it is necessary to refer to that particular statement of a program from some other part of the program.

Statement numbers should be used with every statement. (True or False)

- -

False

4.08 One of the most common uses of statement numbers is to provide control statements with a way to direct the computer to a statement other than the next sequential one.

Statement numbers are very often used with _____ statements.

- -

control

THE GO TO STATEMENT

The first control statement which we will discuss is the GO TO. A GO TO statement has the form

GO TO statement number

For example, the statement,

GO TO 20

will instruct the computer to branch to the statement numbered 20.

Example:

```
20 READ,SIDE
   .....
   .....
   .....
   GO TO 20
```

4.09 In the above example, after executing the statement,

GO TO 20

statement _____ will be executed.

- -

20

4.10 The GO TO statement provides an unconditional branch. The GO TO statement usually appears at the end of a series of statements, and serves to direct the computer to some other part of the program.

The GO TO statement employs _____ branching.

- -

unconditional

The sample program presented below utilizes all of the FORTRAN statements introduced thus far which are:

Assignment
READ
PRINT
STOP
END
GO TO

4.11 Study the program below:

Note: The numbers in parentheses in front of the statements are not part of the program, but are used for line identification.

```
(1)  2  READ,SIDE
(2)     AREA=SIDE*SIDE
(3)     PRINT,SIDE,AREA
(4)     GO TO 2
(5)     STOP
(6)     END
```

The data list for the above program is

4.8, 3.2, 0.0

What are the first eight numbered lines that will be executed?

- -

(1) (2) (3) (4) (1) (2) (3) (4)

4.12 The next series of frames refers to the sample program in the frame above.

In the PRINT statement, you will notice that the value of SIDE as well as that of AREA is called for. This outputting of input data is called echoing. When the programmer requests input information to be printed with his output solutions, he is said to be _____.

- -

echoing

4.13 How many Assignment statements are there in the program?

- -

one   AREA=SIDE*SIDE

4.14 Are there any statement numbers used in this sample? If so, what are they?

- -

Yes, 2 in line (1) is a statement number

4.15 If there were 100 values in the data list, how many times would the PRINT statement in line (3) be executed?

- -

100 times

4.16 How many times will the STOP statement in line (5) be executed with a data list of ten values?

- -

never (The reader is advised to read the following paragraph before questioning the response.)

The reader should note that although there are no FORTRAN grammar or syntax errors in the sample, there is a serious logic error. The program contains an "infinite loop" since only statements (1) (2) (3) and (4) will be executed until the data list is exhausted and then the computer will generate an error message such as

END OF DATA ENCOUNTERED
or
END OF FILE ENCOUNTERED

What is needed is a way to halt the program. This can be done by the use of a control statement called a conditional branching statement.

THE IF STATEMENT

There are two kinds of IF statements in FORTRAN; arithmetic and logical. Both are conditional control statements. At this point in the text only the logical IF will be discussed; later, the arithmetic IF will be presented.

The logical IF statement is used for cases in which the programmer requires the computer to follow one of two possible paths. When this statement is used, the path to be followed is based on the result of a condition which is tested and found to be true or false.

4.17 The logical IF statement is a very useful decision making statement. The logical IF statement is constructed as follows: the word IF followed by a condition to be tested (the kinds of conditions usually tested are comparisons of the numeric values of Identifiers) and a complete statement.

For example:

```
IF (TOTAL.EQ.XLOAN) BALNCE=0.0
XINRST=BALNCE*.06
...
...
```

That part of the statement following the word IF contains the _____ to be tested.

- -

condition

The condition (above) to be tested

TOTAL.EQ.XLOAN

must be enclosed in parentheses. .EQ. designates equal (the periods are necessary). The value of TOTAL will be compared to the value of XLOAN; if TOTAL is equal to XLOAN, the statement

BALNCE=0.0

will be executed and the program will continue. If TOTAL is not equal to XLOAN

BALNCE=0.0

will <u>not</u> be executed and the program will continue.

4.18 The IF statement tells the computer to proceed as follows: Test the condition following the word IF; if the condition is satisfied (True), do the statement following the condition; if the condition is not satisfied (False), go to the next statement in sequence.

Only one of _____ paths may be chosen, based on the test of the condition in the IF statement.

- -

two

4.19 Given the following program segment,

```
B=10.0
IF (A.EQ.0.0) A=1.0
QUOT=B/A
PRINT,QUOT
```

If the computer enters this segment with the Identifier A assigned the value of 10.0, QUOT will have what value when the PRINT statement is executed?

- -

1.0

4.20 If the computer entered the program segment in the last frame with A equal to 0.0, what value of QUOT would be printed?

- -

10.0

The program segment in the last two frames would be flow charted as follows:

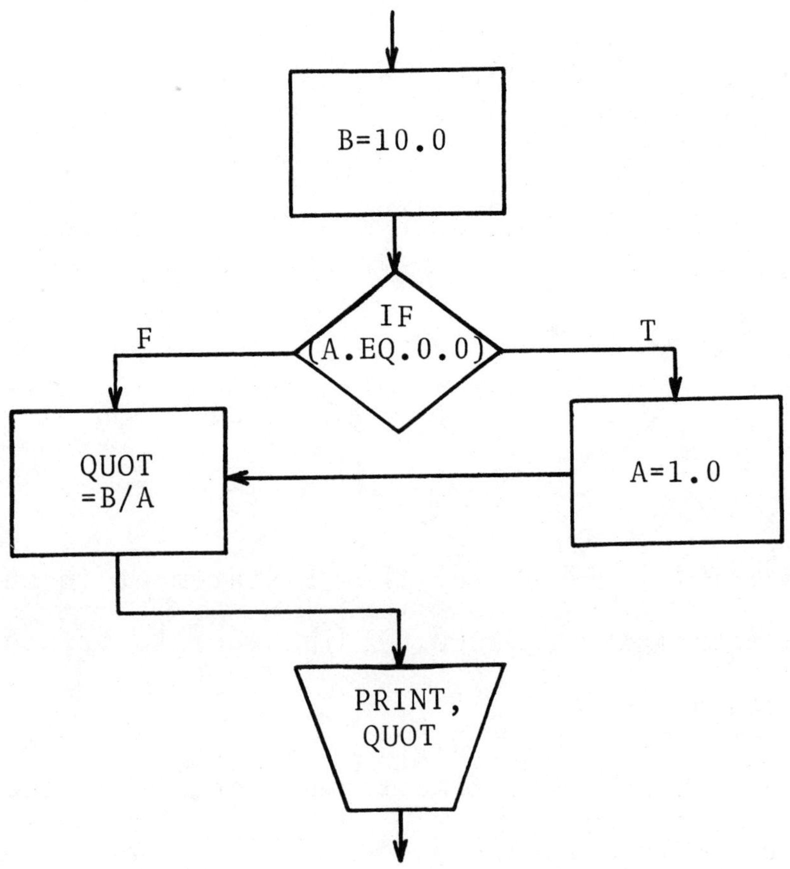

Note: For convenience, the two distinct branches of the IF statement will sometimes be referred to as the true branch and the false branch.

4.21 The computer's ability to follow one of two possible paths (the IF statement) is called conditional branching. When an IF statement is executed, the computer will branch upon testing the condition following the word IF.

Given the following statements,

```
.....
IF (SIDE.EQ.1000.0) STOP
AREA=SIDE*SIDE
PRINT,AREA
.....
```

what value of SIDE will cause the STOP statement to be executed?

- -

1000.0

4.22 Notice carefully the use of the IF statement in checking the condition (SIDE.EQ.1000.0), in order to branch to the STOP statement.

Each branch of an IF statement must contain another FORTRAN statement. (True or False)

- -

True

4.23 The form of the IF statement must be followed exactly: the word IF followed by a condition to be tested; followed by the true branch; followed by the false branch.

The IF statement consists of the word IF and a _____ to be tested, the true branch, and the false branch.

- -

condition

Adding a logical IF statement to our "area of a square" program, we now have,

```
7  READ,SIDE
   IF(SIDE.EQ.0.0) STOP
   AREA=SIDE*SIDE
   PRINT,SIDE,AREA
   GO TO 7
   END
```

data list 4.8, 3.2, 0.0

Study the previous program carefully and notice these points.

1) The word IF, which indicates that the statement involves a decision.
2) The condition (SIDE.EQ.0.0) on which the decision is made, which must be True or False.
3) The statement that is to be executed if the condition is true is STOP.
4) The statement that is executed if the condition is false is AREA=SIDE*SIDE.

A complete summary of the major topics discussed in the text to this point is contained in the sample program that follows. Study it carefully.

SAMPLE PROGRAM

Area of a Square

The program illustrating the flow chart and corresponding FORTRAN statements is shown below. Notice that more than one data item is to be processed and each data item is to be tested.

FLOW CHART:

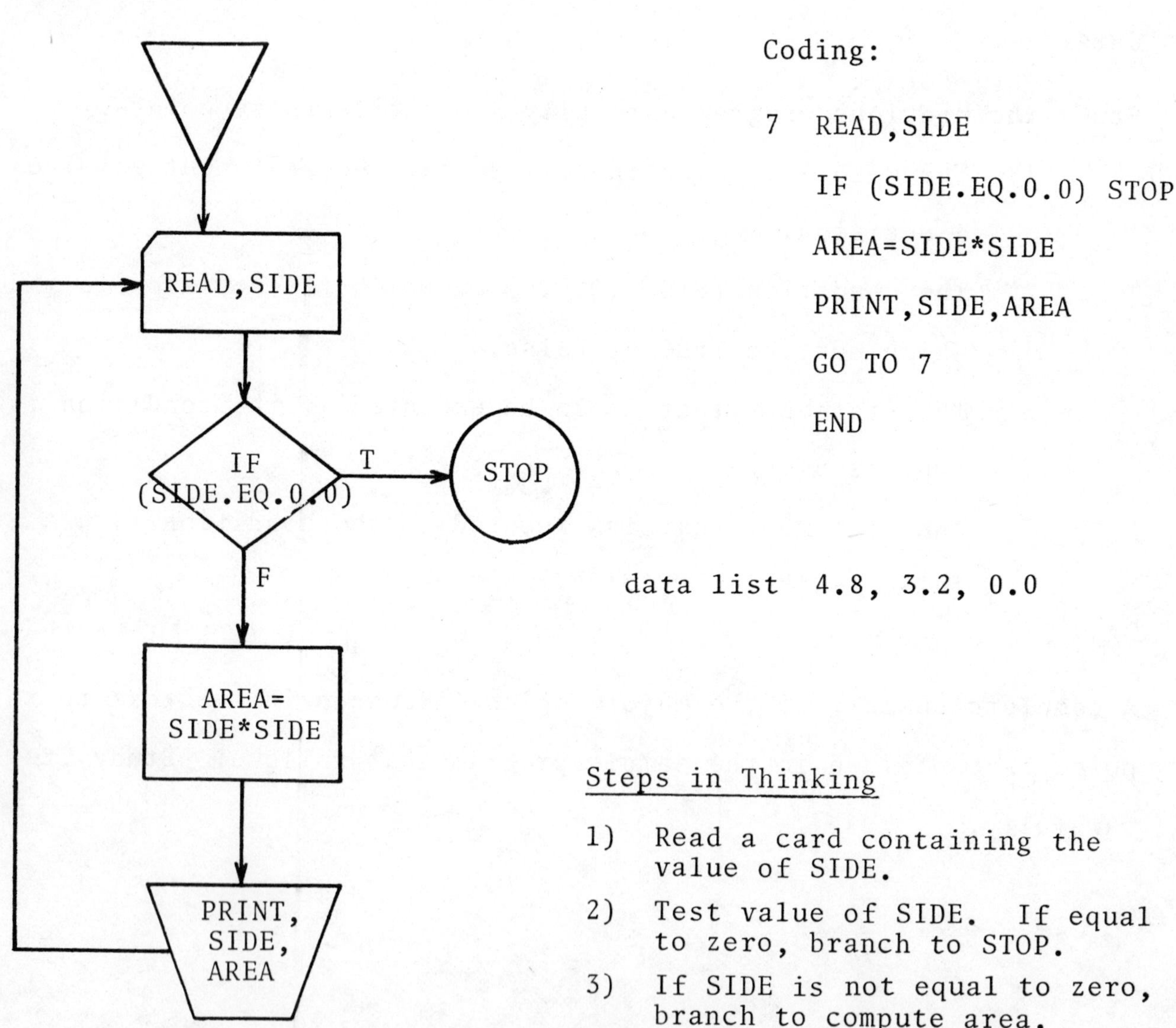

Coding:

```
7  READ,SIDE
   IF (SIDE.EQ.0.0) STOP
   AREA=SIDE*SIDE
   PRINT,SIDE,AREA
   GO TO 7
   END
```

data list 4.8, 3.2, 0.0

Steps in Thinking

1) Read a card containing the value of SIDE.
2) Test value of SIDE. If equal to zero, branch to STOP.
3) If SIDE is not equal to zero, branch to compute area.
4) PRINT information.
5) Go back and read another card.

Note: The GO TO statement may be indicated by simply connecting one flow chart symbol to another.

The following sequence of frames refer to the preceding sample program.

4.24 Which statement calculates the area of the square?

- -

AREA=SIDE*SIDE

4.25 How many times is it executed?

- -

2

4.26 How many times is the PRINT statement executed?

- -

2

4.27 How many times is the READ statement executed?

- -

3

4.28 After the READ statement is executed the third time, what is the value of SIDE?

- -

zero

4.29 When the value of SIDE is <u>not</u> zero, is the condition in the IF statement true or false?

- -

False

4.30 When the condition in the IF statement is false, which statement is executed next?

- -

AREA=SIDE*SIDE

4.31 When the value of SIDE is zero, is the condition in the IF statement true or false?

- -

True

4.32 When the condition in the IF statement is true, which statement is executed?

- -

STOP

Up to this point the .EQ. (symbol for equal) has been the only operator used to test a relation between two quantities in the condition of an IF statement. The following is a more complete list of relational operators that may be used in the condition of an IF statement.

SYMBOL	MEANING
.EQ.	Equal to
.NE.	Not equal to
.GT.	Greater than
.LT.	Less than
.GE.	Greater than or equal to
.LE.	Less than or equal to

4.33 Any of the above relational operators can be used to exercise control over a decision in FORTRAN. Given the following program segment:

```
IF(S.LE.0.0) STOP
A=S*S
PRINT,S,A
...
```

what value of S will cause the STOP statement to be executed?

- -

zero or any negative value

In a condition such as

```
(A.LT.B)
```

the "less than" is called the relational operator and A and B are called operands. In FORTRAN the operands may be any legal FORTRAN expression. Some examples of legal conditions are:

```
(X.LT.Y)
(A+B.EQ.7.0)
(I.LT.9)
(S*(X+Y).GT.17.3)
(KARON.GE.MARIE)
(BILL.NE.BETTY)
```

In a FORTRAN condition both operands should be of the same mode, thus (X.EQ.0) is illegal.

The statement following the condition may be any executable statement except a logical IF or DO statement. DO statements will be discussed in the next chapter.

CHAPTER FOUR TEST

PART 1. Fill in the blanks with the letter of the appropriate entry on the right. Use each answer only once.

_____ (1)	Assignment statement	(a)	GO TO
_____ (2)	Input statement	(b)	IF (J.GT.26)
_____ (3)	Statement number	(c)	SIDE-10.5
_____ (4)	Last executable statement	(d)	PRINT,SIDE,AREA
_____ (5)	Output statement	(e)	2
_____ (6)	Conditional branching	(f)	.LT.
_____ (7)	Unconditional branching	(g)	Y=A+2.1
_____ (8)	Expression	(h)	READ,SIDE
_____ (9)	Relational operator	(i)	SIDE
_____(10)	Identifier	(j)	STOP

PART 2. Find the error in each of the following FORTRAN statements and write it correctly.

a) PRINT A B C

b) READ RATE,COST,TIME

c) IF (A=B) STOP

d) REED,A,B,C

e) GO TO ONE

f) IF (X.LT.Y) THEN GO TO 4

g) PRINT, ARE A, SIDE

h) GO TO STATEMENT 7

i) IF (A.EQUALS.B) STOP

j) A=3.14R**2

PART 3. Indicate whether each of the following statements is True or False.

T ___ (1) The rules against mixed modes apply to the expression contained in the condition of an IF statement.

___ (2) .EQ. is the only operator that may be used to test the condition of an IF statement.

F ___ (3) The logical IF statement may be written so as to provide a three way branch.

___ (4) The statement following the condition of an IF statement is to be executed if the test of the condition is true.

___ (5) A comma must follow the parenthesized expression in an IF statement.

___ (6) An IF statement must have a statement number.

___ (7) Every statement in a FORTRAN program must be assigned a statement number.

___ (8) Printing the data in addition to the solutions is called echoing.

___ (9) The programmer can alter the normal order of execution of statements in a program by the use of a control statement.

___ (10) The GO TO statement is an example of conditional branching in a program.

PART 4. Given the problem: Write a program to find the volume of a box. Use the fact that volume equals length times width times height.

The data list is:

4.7 3.0 6.4 10.7 4.5 8.8 5.2 3.7 6.4 0.0 0.0 0.0

Complete the following flow chart and coding below:

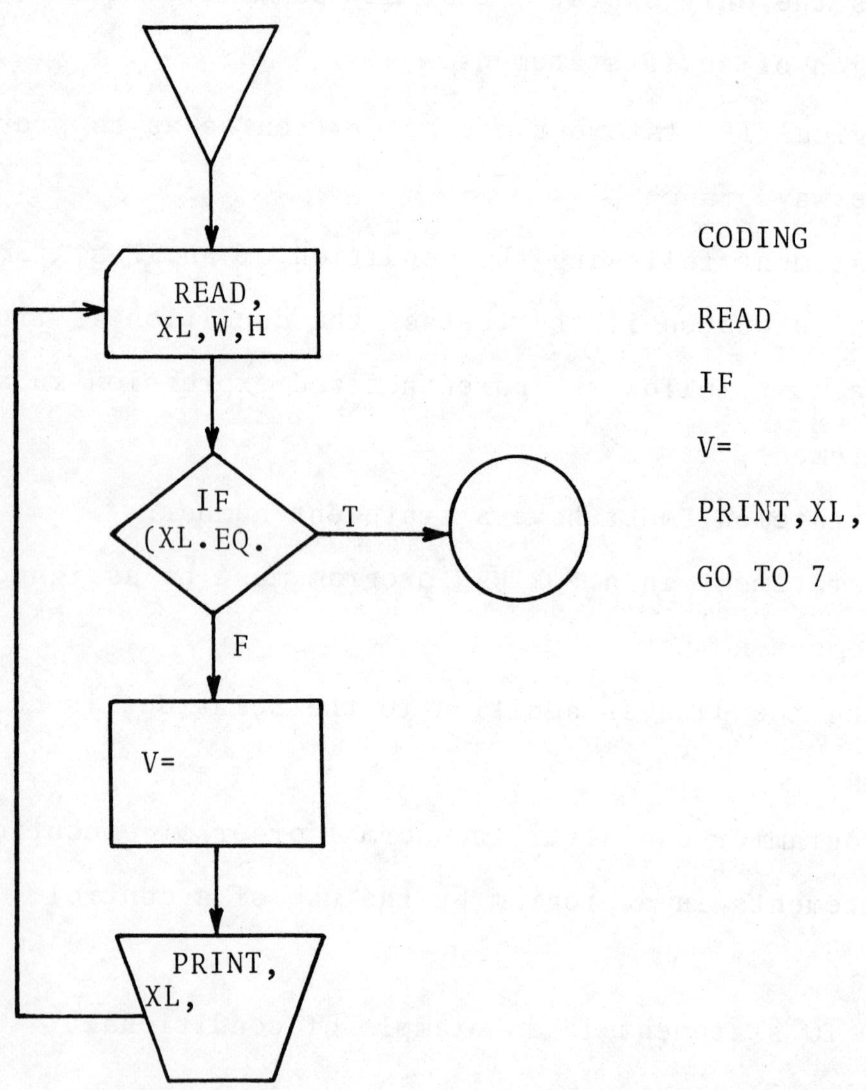

Verify your results before proceeding. See Answers to Tests, Appendix V.

CHAPTER FIVE

LOOPING

A loop in the FORTRAN language is a series of statements to be executed one or more times. In the previous chapter loops were executed with the help of the GO TO statement, and were terminated by the aid of an IF statement. While this technique is workable, it is not convenient for certain types of programs.

In this chapter a new statement called a DO statement will be introduced for the purpose of dealing more effectively with loops.

THE DO STATEMENT

5.01 Previously, the reader saw a discussion of a program that involved control by an IF statement. This program continued to read data, compute the area, and print the solution until a data value of zero was encountered.

This sequence of operations continued until the zero data item was read, and then control branched to the STOP statement. (True or False)

- -

True

5.02 Computer programs will very often involve a series of statements that is to be executed many times. FORTRAN provides the DO statement to control such a loop.

The FORTRAN statement for controlling looping is the _____ statement.

- -

DO

The DO statement not only allows the programmer to have a statement or a series of statements executed repeatedly until a specified condition is satisfied, but it also provides a counter at the same time.

The simplest form of the DO statement is:

DO statement number integer Identifier=positive integer, positive integer

The word DO followed by the statement number of the last statement in the loop, followed in turn by an index definition is a DO statement.

Listed below are three examples of DO statement construction.

```
DO 40 J=1,20
DO 10 I=5,100
DO 26 K=3,33
```

5.03 The DO statement always begins with the word _____.

- -

DO

The index definition (e.g., J=1,20) indicates that the Identifier to the left of the equal sign is set equal to the first quantity on the right of the equal sign for the first pass through the loop, and that the Identifier's value is increased by 1 on each successive pass, until it reaches a value greater than the second quantity on the right of the equal sign.

5.04 The index definition shown above would cause the value of the Identifier J to be increased by _____ on each successive pass through the loop.

- -

1

5.05 The index definition is always made up of an integer Identifier followed by an equal sign and at least two positive integer quantities separated by a comma.

The index definition S=1,100 is a valid index definition. (True or False)

- -

False (S is not an integer Identifier.)

5.06 The DO statement tells the computer to repeatedly execute the series of statements up to and including the statement whose number appears in the DO.

The statement,

```
DO 40 J=1,20
```

will cause the computer to repeatedly execute the statements following the DO up to and including the statement numbered ____.

- -

40

THE CONTINUE STATEMENT

Any FORTRAN statement may be used within a DO loop; however, the loop must not end with a control statement, such as IF or GO TO. To avoid ending a loop in a control statement, a dummy statement is used. This is the CONTINUE statement. The form of the CONTINUE statement is

statement number CONTINUE

5.07 The CONTINUE statement does nothing in the execution of the program; that is, it does not tell the computer to do anything. It merely provides the DO statement with a reference point in a loop.

The following is a valid program. (True or False)

```
      DO 40 J=1,25
      JSQ=J*J
      PRINT,J,JSQ
   40 CONTINUE
      STOP
      END
```

- -

True

Frames 5.08 through 5.11 refer to the following program:

```
(1)       DO 30 J=1,20
(2)       READ,SIDE
(3)       AREA=SIDE*SIDE
(4)       PRINT,SIDE,AREA
(5)    30 CONTINUE
(6)       STOP
(7)       END
```

5.08 How many times will lines (2) through (5) be executed?

- -

20

5.09 How many times will line (6) be executed?

- -

1

5.10 The statements,

```
DO 30 J=1,20
READ,SIDE
```

would direct the computer to read how many values for SIDE from the data list?

- -

20

5.11 How many lines of output will be printed?

- -

20

5.12 It is necessary that the form of the DO statement be strictly observed.

The statement,

```
DO 30,K=1,20
```

is a legal DO statement. (True or False)

- -

False (No comma is permitted after the statement number.)

5.13 The first quantity to the right of the equal sign should be a smaller value than the second quantity, because the index is always counted upward. If this rule is not followed, the loop may cycle once and the computer will proceed to the statement after the statement specified as the last statement in the loop.

The loop described by DO 20 J=10,5 may be executed _____ times.

- -

1 (with J=10)

5.14 A DO loop can be used to generate data within the program. Given the problem: Print a table of the area of the squares whose sides vary from 1 through 25:

```
(1)       DO 30 J=1,25
(2)       IAREA=J*J
(3)       PRINT,J,IAREA
(4)    30 CONTINUE
(5)       STOP
(6)       END
```

What line numbers are included in the DO loop?

---

(1), (2), (3), (4)

5.15 How many times will the loop be executed?

25

5.16 What line number will be processed after the loop is executed the specified number of times?

---

(5)

5.17 When the loop is executed, the first value printed for IAREA will be _____.

1

5.18 When the loop is executed the fourth time, the value printed out for IAREA will be _____.

- -

16

5.19 The set of statements beginning with the DO statement and including all subsequent statements through the statement referred to in the DO itself is called the <u>range</u> of the DO. Which line numbers in frame 5.14 constitute the range of the DO?

- -

(1), (2), (3), (4)

5.20 When the loop has been executed the required number of times, and the index exceeds the value specified by the second quantity in the index definition, the loop is said to be <u>satisfied</u>. The loop in frame 5.14 is satisfied when J=_____.

- -

26

The flow chart symbol for the DO statement,

DO 10 J=1,25

has three sections:

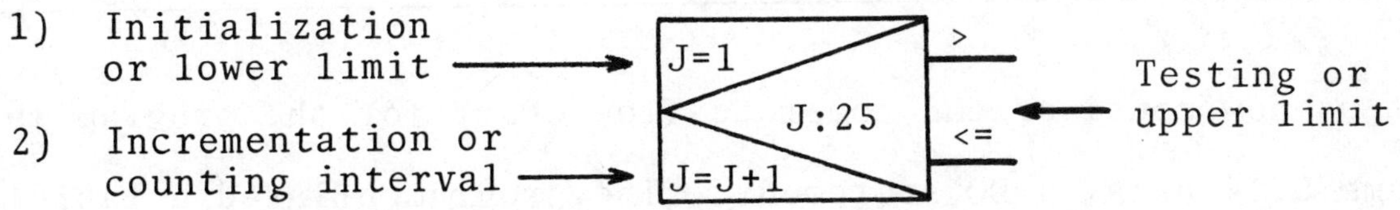

1) Initialization or lower limit → J=1

2) Incrementation or counting interval → J=J+1

J:25 (> / <=) ← Testing or upper limit

5.21 The first quantity shown to the right of the equal sign in the index definition is called the _____ or _____ _____.

- -

initialization   lower limit

5.22 The second quantity shown to the right of the equal sign is called the upper limit, and is used to _____ the value of the index.

- -

test

5.23 The DO statement,

DO 20 J=1,25

will cause the computer to count upward by intervals of _____.

- -

one

5.24 The counting interval is also called the _____.

- -

increment

Let us now consider the complete flow chart for the program in frame 5.14 using a DO statement. The program printed a table of the area of the squares whose sides varied from 1 through 25.

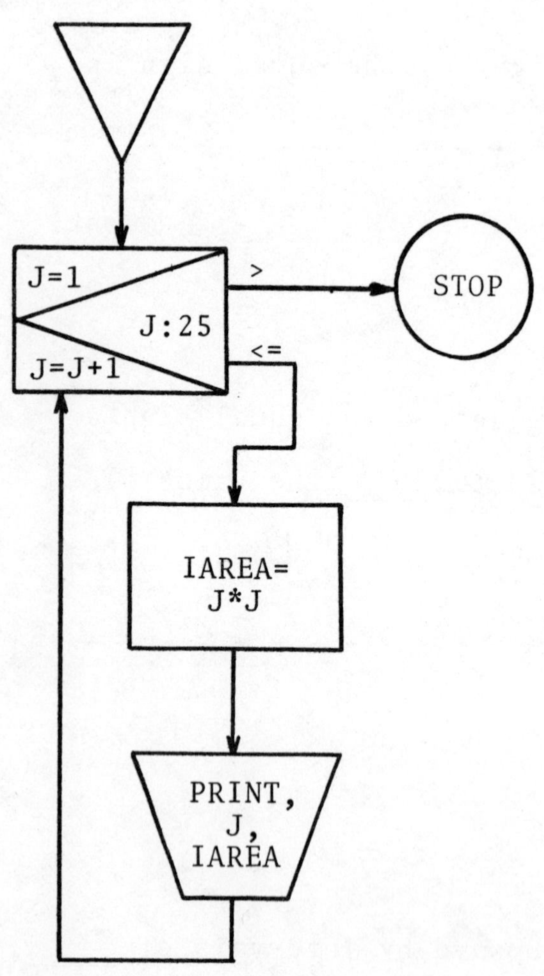

Program begins with J=1

Tests to see if J>25

Since J<25, proceeds to compute area with J=1

IAREA=J*J

Prints values for J and IAREA

Returns to DO statement and increments J by 1

J now equals 2

The loop is repeated

The loop is executed 25 times

Returning to the DO statement after the 25th time, J=25+1=26

Testing again, J>25

Now the computer goes to STOP

5.25 When the loop flow charted on the preceding page is executed the first time, the value for IAREA that will be printed out will be _____.

- -

1

5.26 When the loop is executed the third time, IAREA will equal _____.

- -

9

5.27 When J=26, the computer will proceed to the _____ statement.

- -

STOP

We have demonstrated a DO loop which will increment by one each time the loop completes a cycle.

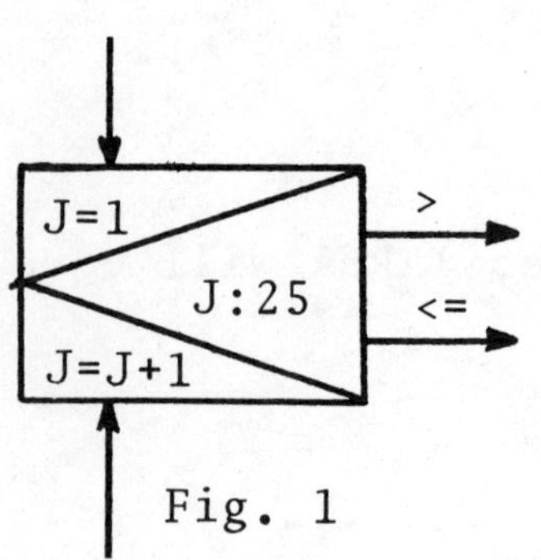

Fig. 1

This statement would provide the loop in Fig. 1:

```
DO 20 J=1,25
```

However, this statement would also provide the identical results:

```
DO 20 J=1,25,1
```

Notice that the third number is 1 and directs the loop to increment by 1 each time through each cycle.

This loop would cycle 25 times.

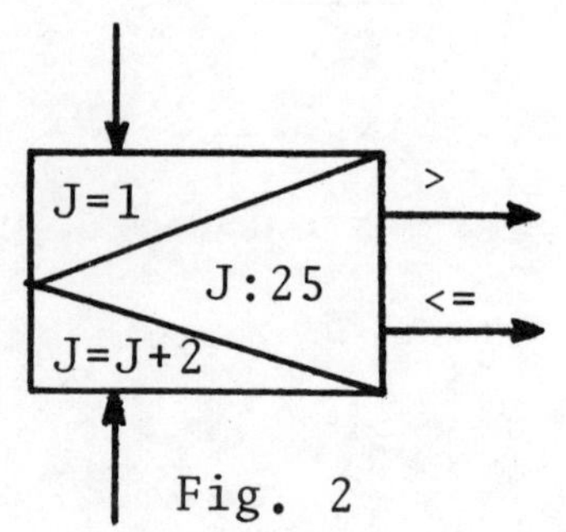

Fig. 2

On the other hand, this statement would provide the loop in Fig. 2:

```
DO 20 J=1,25,2
```

Notice that our third number is 2 and directs the loop to increment by 2 each time through the cycle.

This loop would cycle 13 times.

It is possible to increment by 1, 2, 3, 4, 5, etc., adding the appropriate integer as the third number in the DO statement.

5.28 Assume our DO statement was constructed as follows:

DO 20 J=1,10,2

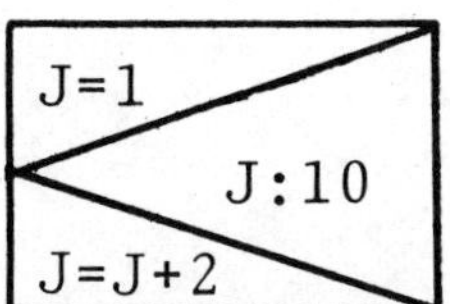

The number of times the loop would be executed would be _____.

- -

5

Note: The values for J would be 1, 3, 5, 7, 9.

5.29 The following DO statements will provide identical results:

(a) DO 20 J=1,10

(b) DO 20 J=1,10,1

The third number in statement (b) is therefore unnecessary in this statement. (True or False)

- -

True

5.30 In this example,

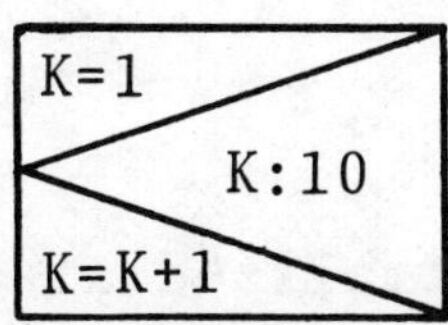

the loop will no longer be executed when K is:

(a) 9 (b) 10 (c) 11

- -

(c) 11

5.31 Given the DO statement,

```
DO 60 K=2,7,2
```

the largest value for K processed by the loop will be _____.

- -

6

5.32 It is permissible to initialize the DO statement at some value other than one.

```
DO 10 J=40,50
```

is a valid statement. (True or False)

- -

True

5.33 Initialization of a DO statement is accomplished by inserting the required positive integer immediately to the right of the equal sign.

Which of the statements below are valid?

(a) DO 20 L=0,5
(b) DO 10 K=-10,10
(c) DO 30 I=.5,5

- -

None   The DO must be initialized at a positive integer value. Note: Some versions of FORTRAN allow initialization at zero. Although the index definition in the DO statement is restricted to positive integer values, it is possible to use the DO statement to generate fractional or negative data by writing additional statements into the program.

Let us re-examine the elements of the DO statement and summarize:

DO 20 J=1,10,2

COMMAND	DO	The command DO indicates that the computer is to execute this statement and all other statements up to and including statement number 20.
RANGE	20	The range of the DO includes the statements that are to be executed repeatedly. The last statement must be identified by number, and this statement number follows the command DO.
INDEX	J	Each DO statement has associated with it an integer Identifier chosen by the programmer and used to keep track of the number of times the statements within the range have been executed.
INITIAL VALUE	1	The programmer exercises complete control over the indexing by indicating the first value.
TEST VALUE	10	Upon each execution of the statements in the range of the DO, the value of the index is compared with the test value, which in this case is ten. When the index exceeds the test value, the DO is considered satisfied and control passes outside the range of the DO. Control would thus pass to the statement following the last statement in the range.
INCREMENT VALUE	2	Another control over the index is obtained by specifying how much the index is to increase upon each execution of the statements in the range - in this case, 2. If no value is specified for incrementation, it is understood that the increment is to be 1.

CHAPTER FIVE TEST

PART 1. Study the following program and then answer the questions below.

```
(1)        DO 20 J=2,50,2
(2)        FAHR=J
(3)        CENT=(5.0/9.0)*(FAHR-32.0)
(4)        PRINT,FAHR,CENT
(5)     20 CONTINUE
(6)        STOP
(7)        END
```

a) At what value is index variable initialized?

b) What is the test value?

c) What is the value of the indexing increment?

d) What is the condition that is tested each time the loop is executed?

e) How many lines of output will be printed?

f) How many Identifier values will be printed on each line?

g) Is the first pair of parentheses in line (3) necessary?

h) Is the second pair of parentheses in line (3) necessary?

i) Revise the statement in line (1) so that the loop will process the Fahrenheit values from 32 to 212 in steps of 2.

j) What is the effect on the program if lines (5) and (6) are interchanged?

PART 2. The following program contains errors. Detect these errors and rewrite the program correctly.

```
    DO 100, J=1,20
    S=J
    AREA=S**2
    VOL=AREA*S
    PRINT S,AREA,VOL
100 CONTINUE
    END
    STOP
```

PART 3. Develop a program which prints two columns of output. The first column should contain the integers from 1 to 15 and the second column should contain the sum of the integers less than or equal to the integer in the first column. The output should be

```
 1     1   (since 1=1)
 2     3   (since 3=1+2)
 3     6   (since 6=1+2+3)
 4    10   (since 10=1+2+3+4)
 .     .
 .     .
 .     .
14   105
15   120
```

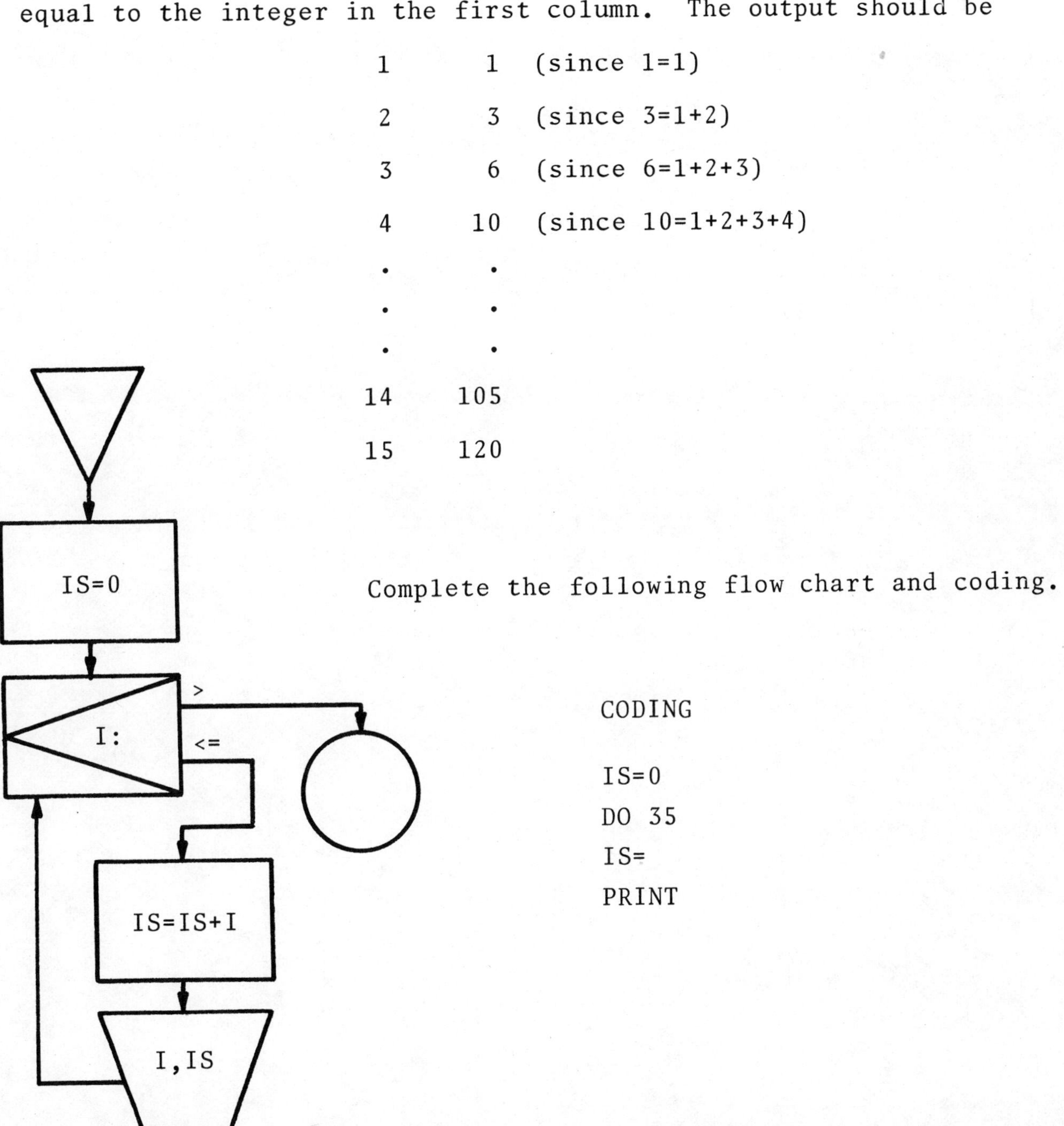

Complete the following flow chart and coding.

CODING

```
IS=0
DO 35
IS=
PRINT
```

Verify your results before proceeding to the next chapter. See Answers to Tests, Appendix V.

CHAPTER SIX

PROGRAM ASSEMBLY AND SAMPLE PROGRAMS

In this chapter, two complete sample programs and three partial programs will be presented. In addition, all of the necessary steps in the sequence of preparing and processing the programs will be demonstrated: analyzing, flow charting, coding, preparing input, and obtaining output.

ANALYZING THE PROBLEM

After the problem is read, a general procedure for solution must be determined. Thought must be given to such questions as

> Can data be generated or must they be supplied?
>
> Is an arithmetic formula needed? Is it used once or can it be used many times by placing it within a DO loop?
>
> How can the program execution be terminated?
>
> What information will be desired in the print out of the solution?

FLOW CHARTING

In Chapter One, the idea of representing the steps of a problem by the use of a flow chart was introduced. In Chapters Four and Five, this technique was employed to demonstrate the manner in which control statements such as the IF and DO are used to alter the sequence in which the computer executes the various statements of the program.

Since the flow chart technique so conveniently demonstrates visually the logical sequence of steps to be performed in a problem, the reader is strongly advised to construct a flow chart for each problem he attempts before coding.

The beginner will find it instructive to follow a few numerical values through the step-by-step flow of the problem to assure, before coding, that the sequencing is correct and that the execution can terminate.

Although almost any geometric figures can be used to indicate the type of activity to be performed, the reader will find that the following set of geometric figures recommended for FORTRAN will be most useful.

FLOW CHART SYMBOLS

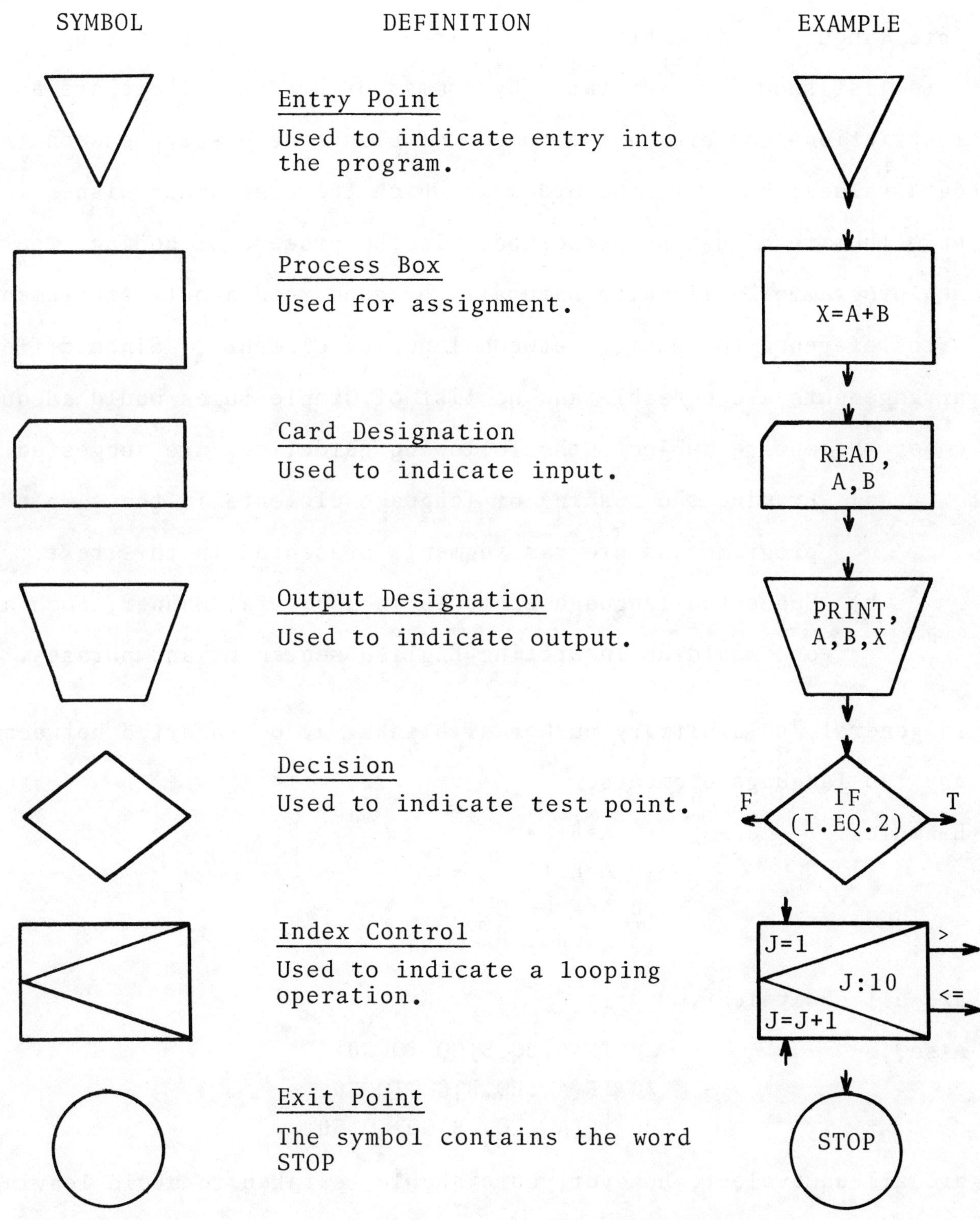

SYMBOL
DEFINITION
EXAMPLE
Entry Point
Used to indicate entry into the program.
Process Box
Used for assignment.
X=A+B
Card Designation
Used to indicate input.
READ, A,B
Output Designation
Used to indicate output.
PRINT, A,B,X
Decision
Used to indicate test point.
F
IF (I.EQ.2)
T
Index Control
Used to indicate a looping operation.
J=1
J:10
J=J+1
>
<=
Exit Point
The symbol contains the word STOP
STOP

CODING

Coding consists of translating the logical steps in the flow chart into language statements. The individual values constituting the data list should be separated by commas or blanks. There are no restrictions concerning the number of blanks necessary between the data values; however, the order in which the programmer wishes to have them read must be preserved. In the process of coding, the new programmer will quite naturally be concerned about requirements with reference to spacing between language elements. Since different arrangements are possible and no list of simple rules would adequately cover the entire subject, the following guidelines are suggested.

a) Examine the spacing of language elements in the sample programs and program segments presented in this text;

b) Space the language elements in a natural manner, such as one would do in writing English sentences and phrases.

In general, an arbitrary number of blanks may be inserted between any two language elements.

Examples:

```
10 A=B+C
10 A=B +C
10 A = B+ C
10 A= B + C
```

are all equivalent.

Also,

```
20 IF(A.EQ.B)GO TO 30
20 IF(A .EQ.B)GO TO 30
20 IF(A .EQ. B)GO TO 30
```

are all equivalent, however, care should be taken to avoid leaving blanks between digits of a number: a zero may be supplied in the blank by some versions of FORTRAN.

It is recommended that commercially prepared coding sheets, which picture the card columns to be punched, be used as an aid in writing the programs. Such a sheet appears below.

COMM.	STATEMENT NUMBER				CONT.																											IDENTIFICATION SEQUENCE							
1	2	3	4	5	6	7	8	9	10	11	12	13	14	15	16	17	18	19	20	21	22	23	24	25	26	66	67	68	69	70	71	72	73	74	75	76	77	78	79	80

1 2 3 4 5 6 7 8 9 10 11 12 13 14 15 16 17 18 19 20 21 22 23 24 25 26 66 67 68 69 70 71 72 73 74 75 76 77 78 79 80

THE HOLLERITH CARD

ABCDEFGHIJKLMNOPQRSTUVWXYZ 0123456789 @%*<-#,$./&+_)¢|>:;¬'?"=!(

ISC/PRYOR 5081-10

Hollerith Card with Character Code

The Hollerith card is a standard size card with most cards having a corner cut for ease in hand sorting. The standard card has 80 columns. Each character on the key punch machine uses one column for representation. As shown on the card above, a character may be represented by one, two or three punches in a particular column.

In FORTRAN, only program information punched in the first seventy-two columns of the eighty column Hollerith card is processed. Information punched in columns seventy-three to eighty is for the programmer's reference only and is not processed by the computer. Therefore, the programmer must confine the instructions he wants processed to the first seventy-two columns on the coding sheet.

Of the first seventy-two columns, columns one to five are reserved for statement numbers. Column six is reserved for a special function which will be discussed in Chapter Nine. Columns seven to seventy-two are available for the statements constituting the program. The FORTRAN statement itself should be written beginning in column seven of the coding sheet.

C ← FOR COMMENT | STATEMENT NUMBER | CONTINUATION | FORTRAN STATEMENT | IDENTIFICATION

```
0 0 0 0 0 0 0 0 0 0 0 0 0 0 0 0 0 0 0 0 0 0 0 0 0 0 0 0 0 0 0 0 0 0 0 0 0 0 0 0 0 0 0 0 0 0 0 0 0 0 0 0 0 0 0 0 0 0 0 0 0 0 0 0 0 0 0 0 0 0 0 0 0 0 0 0 0 0 0 0
1 2 3 4 5 6 7 8 9 10 11 12 13 14 15 16 17 18 19 20 21 22 23 24 25 26 27 28 29 30 31 32 33 34 35 36 37 38 39 40 41 42 43 44 45 46 47 48 49 50 51 52 53 54 55 56 57 58 59 60 61 62 63 64 65 66 67 68 69 70 71 72 73 74 75 76 77 78 79 80
1 1 1 1 1 1 1 1 1 1 1 1 1 1 1 1 1 1 1 1 1 1 1 1 1 1 1 1 1 1 1 1 1 1 1 1 1 1 1 1 1 1 1 1 1 1 1 1 1 1 1 1 1 1 1 1 1 1 1 1 1 1 1 1 1 1 1 1 1 1 1 1 1 1 1 1 1 1 1 1
2 2 2 2 2 2 2 2 2 2 2 2 2 2 2 2 2 2 2 2 2 2 2 2 2 2 2 2 2 2 2 2 2 2 2 2 2 2 2 2 2 2 2 2 2 2 2 2 2 2 2 2 2 2 2 2 2 2 2 2 2 2 2 2 2 2 2 2 2 2 2 2 2 2 2 2 2 2 2 2
3 3 3 3 3 3 3 3 3 3 3 3 3 3 3 3 3 3 3 3 3 3 3 3 3 3 3 3 3 3 3 3 3 3 3 3 3 3 3 3 3 3 3 3 3 3 3 3 3 3 3 3 3 3 3 3 3 3 3 3 3 3 3 3 3 3 3 3 3 3 3 3 3 3 3 3 3 3 3 3
4 4 4 4 4 4 4 4 4 4 4 4 4 4 4 4 4 4 4 4 4 4 4 4 4 4 4 4 4 4 4 4 4 4 4 4 4 4 4 4 4 4 4 4 4 4 4 4 4 4 4 4 4 4 4 4 4 4 4 4 4 4 4 4 4 4 4 4 4 4 4 4 4 4 4 4 4 4 4 4
5 5 5 5 5 5 5 5 5 5 5 5 5 5 5 5 5 5 5 5 5 5 5 5 5 5 5 5 5 5 5 5 5 5 5 5 5 5 5 5 5 5 5 5 5 5 5 5 5 5 5 5 5 5 5 5 5 5 5 5 5 5 5 5 5 5 5 5 5 5 5 5 5 5 5 5 5 5 5 5
6 6 6 6 6 6 6 6 6 6 6 6 6 6 6 6 6 6 6 6 6 6 6 6 6 6 6 6 6 6 6 6 6 6 6 6 6 6 6 6 6 6 6 6 6 6 6 6 6 6 6 6 6 6 6 6 6 6 6 6 6 6 6 6 6 6 6 6 6 6 6 6 6 6 6 6 6 6 6 6
7 7 7 7 7 7 7 7 7 7 7 7 7 7 7 7 7 7 7 7 7 7 7 7 7 7 7 7 7 7 7 7 7 7 7 7 7 7 7 7 7 7 7 7 7 7 7 7 7 7 7 7 7 7 7 7 7 7 7 7 7 7 7 7 7 7 7 7 7 7 7 7 7 7 7 7 7 7 7 7
8 8 8 8 8 8 8 8 8 8 8 8 8 8 8 8 8 8 8 8 8 8 8 8 8 8 8 8 8 8 8 8 8 8 8 8 8 8 8 8 8 8 8 8 8 8 8 8 8 8 8 8 8 8 8 8 8 8 8 8 8 8 8 8 8 8 8 8 8 8 8 8 8 8 8 8 8 8 8 8
9 9 9 9 9 9 9 9 9 9 9 9 9 9 9 9 9 9 9 9 9 9 9 9 9 9 9 9 9 9 9 9 9 9 9 9 9 9 9 9 9 9 9 9 9 9 9 9 9 9 9 9 9 9 9 9 9 9 9 9 9 9 9 9 9 9 9 9 9 9 9 9 9 9 9 9 9 9 9 9
1 2 3 4 5 6 7 8 9 10 11 12 13 14 15 16 17 18 19 20 21 22 23 24 25 26 27 28 29 30 31 32 33 34 35 36 37 38 39 40 41 42 43 44 45 46 47 48 49 50 51 52 53 54 55 56 57 58 59 60 61 62 63 64 65 66 67 68 69 70 71 72 73 74 75 76 77 78 79 80
HACKETT 888157
```

The data list, on the other hand, may utilize all of the columns one to eighty. Individual data values may be punched anywhere in the eighty columns of data cards as long as the order in which the programmer wishes to have them read is preserved. There are no restrictions concerning the number of blanks required between data values, but no blanks may appear within a number. Listing data at the bottom of the coding sheet is an aid in checking the READ statement.

6.01 Statements for a FORTRAN program are punched on a keypunch machine. FORTRAN statements are punched one statement per card. The following card is punched correctly. (True or False)

```
 20 A=A+1.0   STOP
```

- -

False   Only one statement is allowed per card, (except when the logical IF is the first statement).

6.02 The following card is punched correctly. (True or False)

```
AREA=SIDE**2.0
```

- -

False   The statement should begin in column seven.

Statement numbers may be punched anywhere in the first five columns of the Hollerith card. However, the safest procedure is to "right justify" with respect to column five when punching - that is, the last digit should be punched in column five, the next to the last in column four, etc. This is done in order to avoid having the computer provide a zero in unpunched column five and causing an error. Some FORTRAN compilers will not provide a zero, but it is best to eliminate the possibility of an error.

It is also safe practice to confine statement numbers to four digits. Some FORTRAN compilers have a higher limit to the statement number; however, four digits are always safe. It is unlikely that the need for a larger statement number would ever arise.

Here are three statement numbers: 40, 400, and 4000, and how they should be positioned in the first five columns.

```
4000 XLAST=FIRST+DIF*(XN-1.0)
```

```
 400 NEW=NEW+1
```

```
  40 SUM=FIRST+XLAST
```

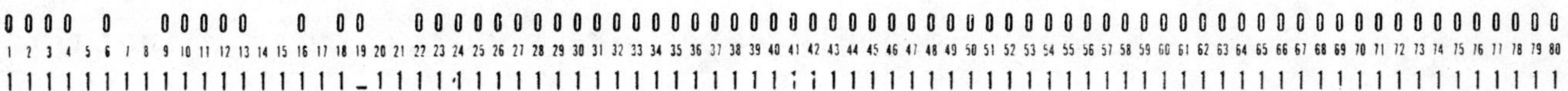

DECK ASSEMBLY

After the program and any required data lists have been punched on the cards, the program is ready for assembling. Every installation has certain cards peculiar to that installation. These cards are placed in the deck in a specified order. One such program assembly is shown below.

```
/END RUN
5.1
/DATA
      END
      STOP
      PRINT, SIDE, AREA
      AREA=SIDE*SIDE
      READ, SIDE
/LOAD WATFOR
/JOB GO
/INPUT
```

Note: Since the deck assembly cards are peculiar to the installation, the reader will have to ascertain which cards are required for the computer he is using.

In analyzing any computer program the programmer must, at some point, answer the question, "Can data be generated or must they be supplied?" Since this question may be difficult for the new programmer to answer, of the two sample programs that follow, one program requires that data be supplied and the other generates the data required. The flow chart, the punched Hollerith cards and the printed output for each program are shown.

Following the sample programs, three partially written programs are presented. By examining the flow charts provided, referring back to the sample programs and using the information the reader now has, he should be able to supply the missing items.

Completion of the partial programs will bring the reader to the stage at which he should attempt to write the programs for problems one through ten in the Practice Problems in Appendix I. Since the beginning programmer is likely to experience difficulties with some of these problems, a number of hints for each problem will be found in Appendix II. An additional aid appears in Appendix III in the form of a series of complete sample programs.

SAMPLE PROGRAM ONE

PROBLEM: Write a program to compute the area of triangles, using the formula, A = 1/2 bh.

FLOW CHART:

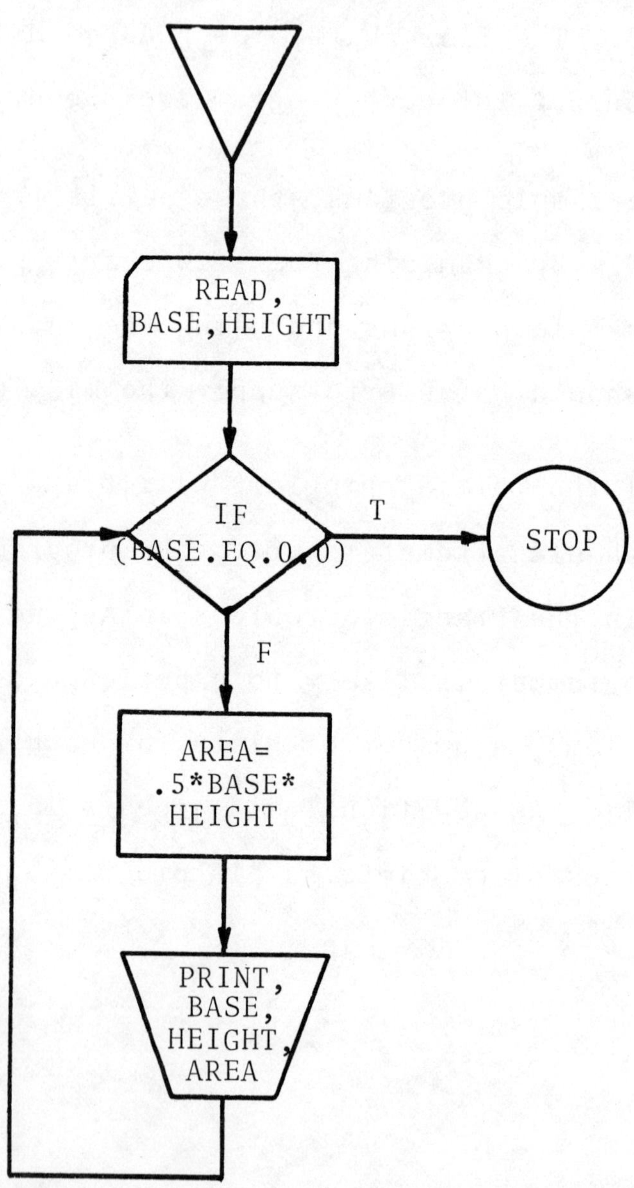

DECK:

```
/END RUN
0.0       0.0
5.89      6.34
6.0       2.5
1.5       3.2
5.0       7.0
3.0       4.0
/DATA
      END
      GO TO 10
      PRINT, BASE , HEIGHT, AREA
      AREA=.5*BASE*HEIGHT
      IF(BASE.EQ.0.0) STOP
   10 READ, BASE, HEIGHT
C     SAMPLE PROGRAM ONE
/LOAD WATFOR
/JOB GO
/INPUT
```

ISC/PRYOR 5081-10

Note: The card

C SAMPLE PROGRAM ONE

is a comment card and is explained in Chapter Seven.

INPUT/OUTPUT:

```
/INPUT
/JOB GO
/LOAD WATFOR
C      SAMPLE PROGRAM ONE
   10 READ, BASE, HEIGHT
      IF(BASE.EQ.0.0) STOP
      AREA=.5*BASE*HEIGHT
      PRINT, BASE , HEIGHT, AREA
      GO TO 10
      END
/DATA
3.0       4.0
5.0       7.0
1.5       3.2
6.0       2.5
5.89      6.34
0.0       0.0
/END RUN
*IN PROGRESS

COMPILE =    0.27  SEC
                          3.000000                              4.000000                              6.000000
                          5.000000                              7.000000                              17.50000
                          1.500000                              3.200000                              2.400000
                          6.000000                              2.500000                              7.500000
                          5.890000                              6.340000                              18.67130

EXEC =    0.05  SEC

*END

*GO
```

SAMPLE PROGRAM TWO

PROBLEM: Write a program to convert yards both into feet and into inches. Print the result as a three column table of yards, feet and inches. Let yards range from 1 to 10.

FLOW CHART:

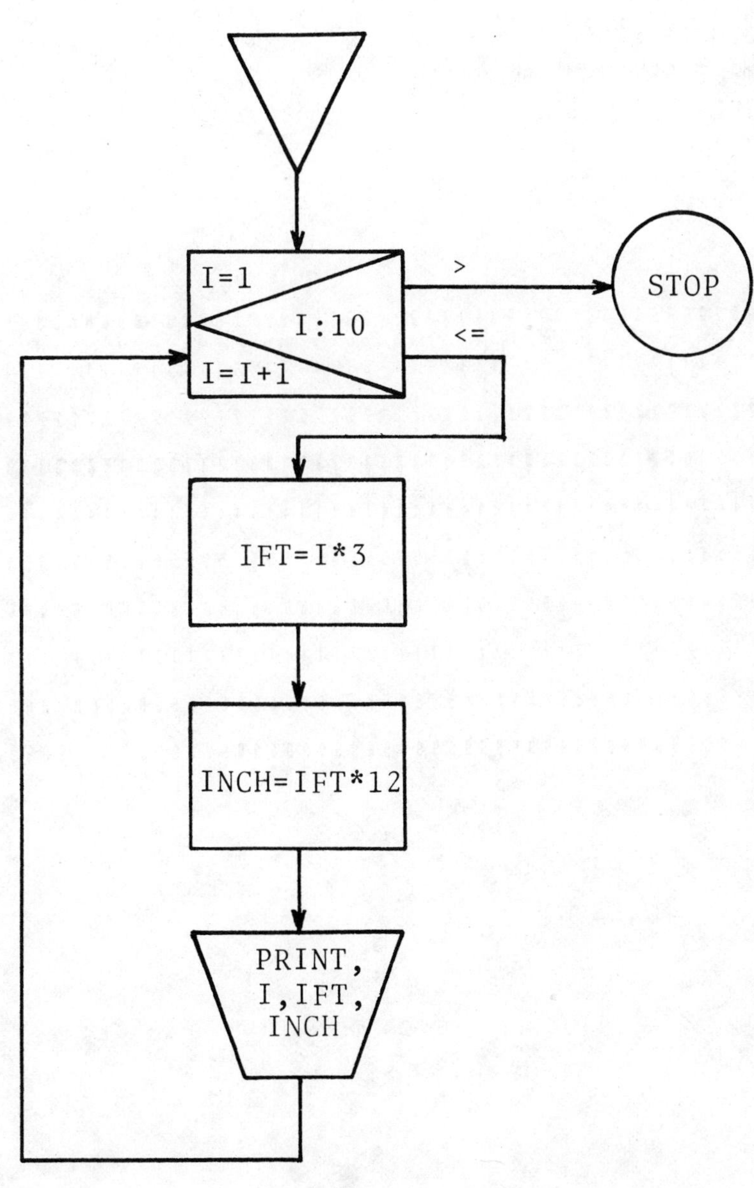

DECK:

```
/END RUN
      END
      STOP
   10 CONTINUE
      PRINT, I, IFT, INCH
      INCH=IFT*12
      IFT=I*3
      DO 10 I=1,10
C     SAMPLE PROGRAM TWO
/LOAD WATFOR
/JOB GO
/INPUT
```

ISC/PRYOR 5081-10

INPUT/OUTPUT:

```
/INPUT
/JOB GO
/LOAD WATFOR
C       SAMPLE PROGRAM TWO
        DO 10 I=1,10
        IFT=I*3
        INCH=IFT*12
        PRINT, I, IFT, INCH
   10   CONTINUE
        STOP
        END
/END RUN
*IN PROGRESS

COMPILE =    0.27  SEC
            1              3             36
            2              6             72
            3              9            108
            4             12            144
            5             15            180
            6             18            216
            7             21            252
            8             24            288
            9             27            324
           10             30            360

EXEC =    0.03  SEC

*END

*GO
```

PARTIAL PROGRAMS

In the next four pages you will have the opportunity of working three partial programs through to completion. Add the missing items to the programs.

SUGGESTIONS

1) Fill in missing items in the incomplete statements.
2) Check the complete program before attempting the next one.
3) If in doubt as to what additions to make, refer to previous portions of this text that contain the information.

PARTIAL PROGRAM ONE

VOLUME OF A CYLINDER

PROBLEM: Write a program to compute the volume of a cylinder given the radius and height. Use the formula $V=\pi r^2h$. Use 3.14 for the value of π.

Complete the program by filling in the missing items in the statements.

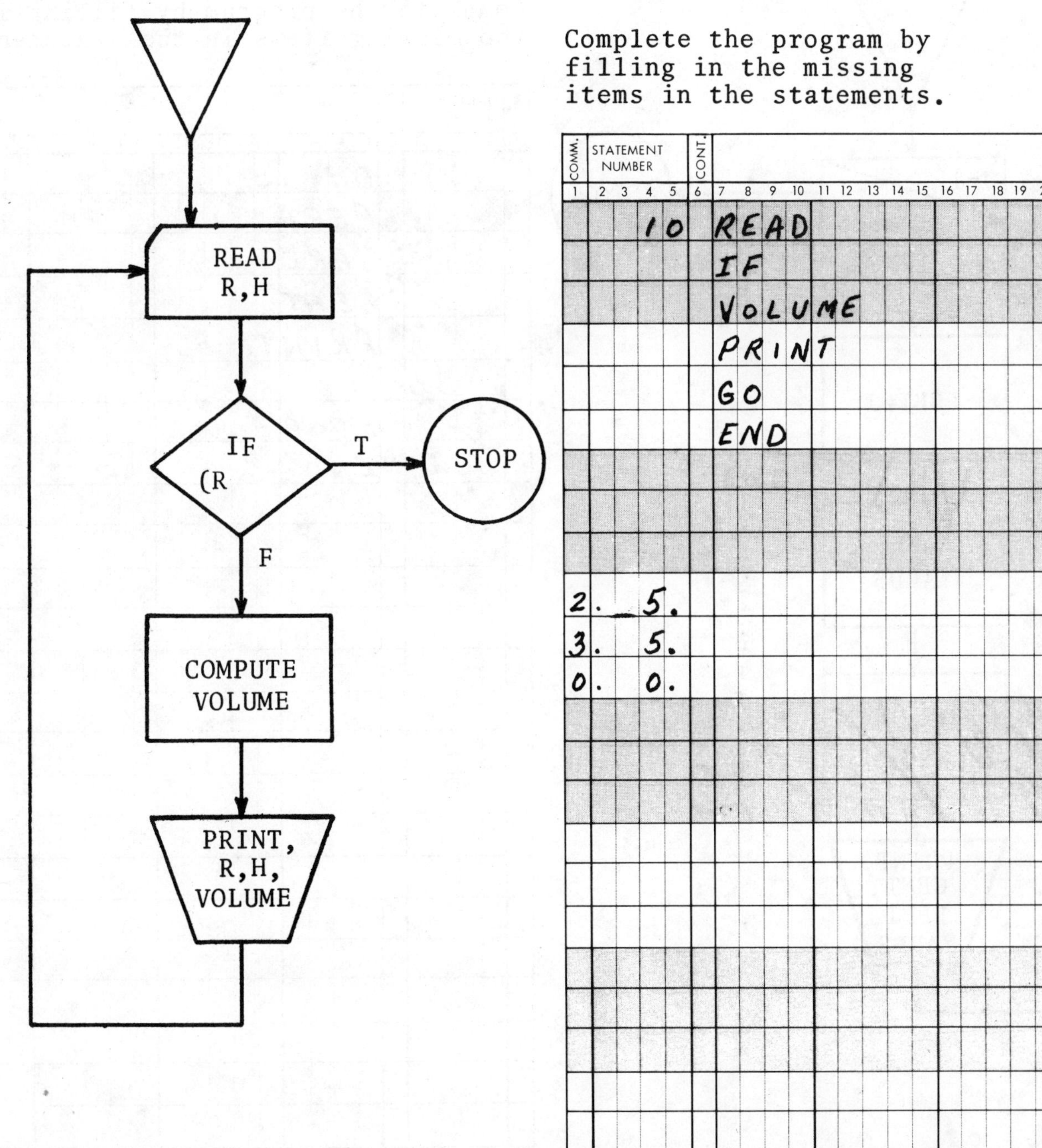

Verify your results.

See solutions in Appendix IV.

PARTIAL PROGRAM TWO

COMPUTING CENTIMETERS AND YARDS FROM FEET

PROBLEM: Write a program to compute centimeters and yards from feet. Feet to vary from 1 to 13 by 1's. One inch = 2.54 centimeters.

Complete the program by filling in the missing items in the statements.

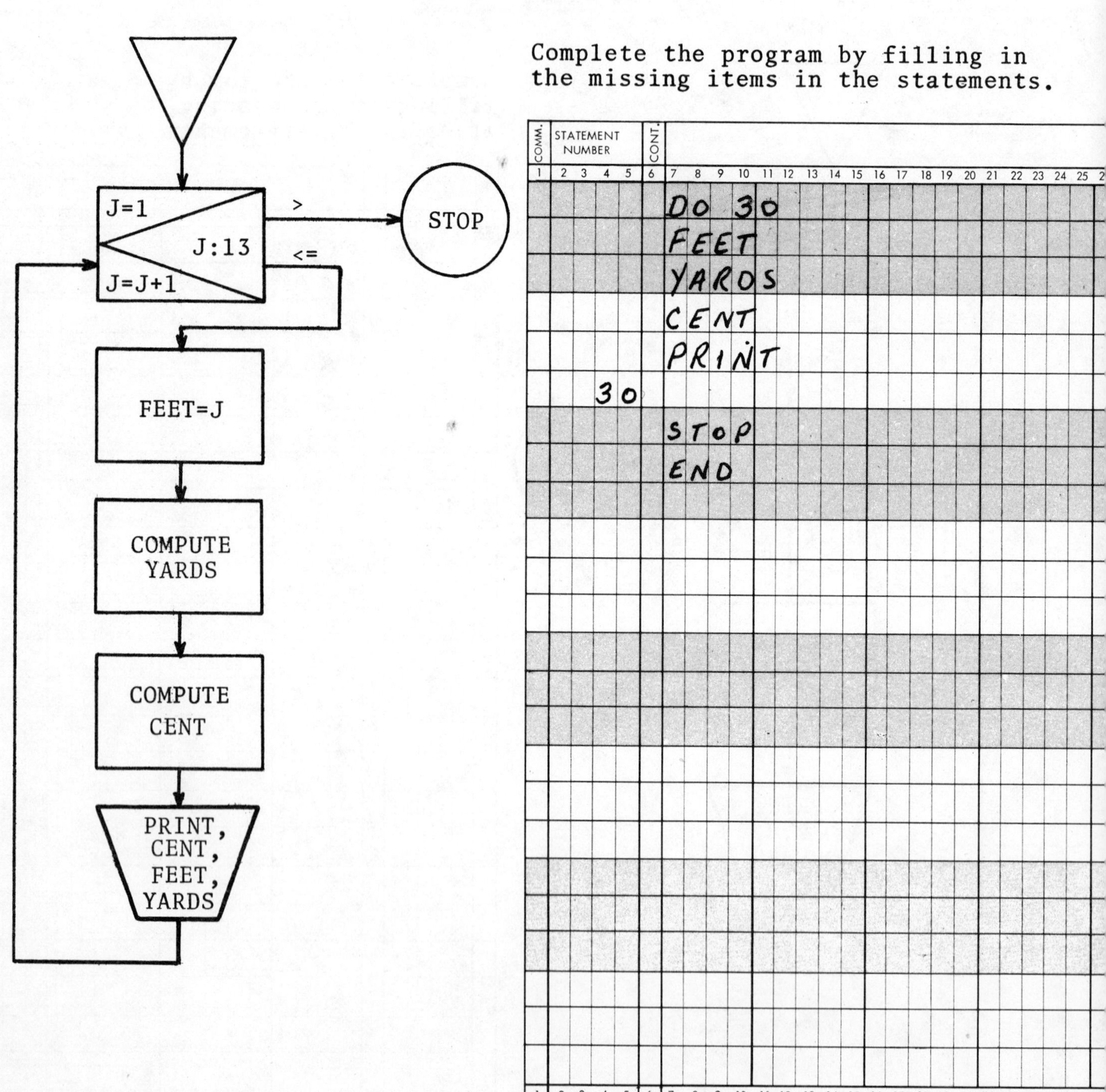

Verify your results. See solutions in Appendix IV.

PARTIAL PROGRAM THREE

SQUARING A NUMBER

PROBLEM: Write a program to square given numbers.

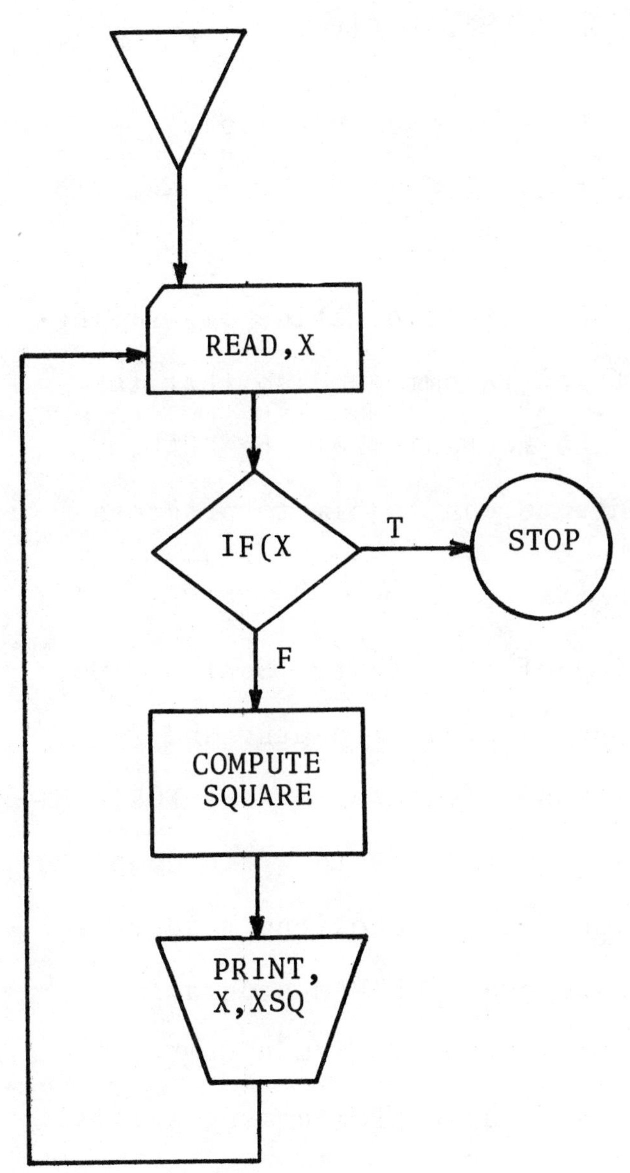

Complete the program by filling in the missing items in the statements.

```
COMM. | STATEMENT NUMBER | CONT. |
1     | 2 3 4 5          | 6     | 7 8 9 10 11 12 13 14 15 16 17 18 19 20 21 22 23 24
    5 READ
      IF
      XSQ=
      PRINT
      GO
      END



5.1
6.3
7.6
8.21
0.0
```

Verify your results.
See Solutions in Appendix IV.

With the introduction to the reader of practice problems and eventually to partial problems, it is now advisable for the reader to write programs of his own. The point has been reached where the reader should be able to compose programs that utilize components of FORTRAN as introduced in Chapters One through Five.

The programs that we have dealt with thus far are relatively uncomplicated and perform simple computations. It might be well to realize that with the material that has thus far been presented a great many programs can be written. The actual practice of writing programs on this plateau of difficulty is recommended so that the reader gains sufficient mastery over the mechanics of the READ, PRINT, Assignment, IF and DO statements to enable him to progress to problems of a more difficult nature.

Chapter Six completes the first section of this text. Section Two treats all of the topics of Section One in greater depth, and introduces the reader to several additional features of the FORTRAN language. Since all of the necessary requirements to write complete FORTRAN programs have been presented in Section One, the reader is strongly advised to write and <u>process</u> several FORTRAN programs before proceeding to Section Two. Learning to program a computer requires the acquisition of many skills. Basic programming skills can be fully mastered only by actual computer programming experience.

SECTION TWO

CHAPTER SEVEN

INPUT/OUTPUT WITH FORMAT

FORMAT FREE INPUT/OUTPUT

In Section One, all programs were developed using FORMAT free input/output statements.

One advantage of using READ and PRINT statements in this manner is that the programmer need not be concerned with specifying to the computer where data will be found on data cards for input or where and how data will be printed for output.

The main disadvantage of FORMAT free input/output statements is that the programmer has no control of the arrangement of his data on input data cards and no control of either the appearance or placement of data on output.

THE FORMAT STATEMENT

In FORTRAN, FORMAT statements may be used to specify where data will be found on input data cards and where and how data should be printed on output. FORMAT statements are specification statements containing a coded set of rules specifying the appearance and form of input/output values. FORMAT statements may be used, at the programmers option, in conjunction with READ and PRINT statements.

READ AND PRINT WITH FORMAT

In previous chapters the statement

```
PRINT,SIDE,AREA
```

has been used. This produced a line of output somewhat like the following.

```
0.2000000E 01    0.4000000E 01
```

The following two statements would produce the same values as output but with a different form.

```
      PRINT7,SIDE,AREA
    7 FORMAT(2F10.4)
```

Output: $_{\wedge\wedge\wedge\wedge}2.0000_{\wedge\wedge\wedge\wedge}$4.0000

(Note: The use of the symbol $_\wedge$ indicates a blank column and will <u>not</u> actually appear in the output.)

When FORMAT statements are used the READ or PRINT statement is followed immediately by a statement number. This statement number refers to a FORMAT statement which specifies where on the input card the data will be found or where and in what form on the output sheet the values should be printed.

THE OUTPUT FORMAT STATEMENT

FORMAT statements will be discussed in depth later in this chapter. At this time we will restrict our discussion to two specific FORMAT statements:

a) FORMAT(F10.4)

b) FORMAT(I10)

Note the construction of statements a and b above.

The word FORMAT is followed by the specification enclosed within parentheses.

In statement a:

The alphabetic character F specifies real mode. The number 10.4, specifies that the values printed will be printed in ten columns called print positions and contain four decimal places. The meaning of F10.4 may be visualized as follows:

sxxxx.xxxx

where s designates sign (plus or minus); x designates a digit and . indicates a decimal point.

Note: sxxxx.xxxx requires 10 print positions.

In statement b:

The alphabetic character I specifies integer mode. The number 10, specifies that the values printed will be right justified in ten columns.

7.01 A FORMAT statement may be used with a PRINT statement to specify the mode and the number of columns to provide for the value of each Identifier listed in the PRINT statement.

In the following statements:

```
      PRINT40,AREA
   40 FORMAT(F10.4)
```

assuming the computed value of AREA to be 25.2, we can expect this information to be printed in real mode. (True or False)

- -

True

Note: The F in the FORMAT statement specifies real numbers.

7.02 The number which identifies the FORMAT statement must appear both in the PRINT statement, and as the statement number placed in front of the word FORMAT.

Given the following statements:

```
      PRINT20,AREA
   20 FORMAT(F10.4)
```

the statement number of the FORMAT statement is _____.

- -

20

7.03 Study this program segment:

```
PRINT20,AREA
20 FORMAT(F10.4)
```

Select the correct answer:

a) _ _ _ 6 5 . 6 4 0 0

b) 6 5 . 6 4 0 0 0 0 0

- -

a

Note: The 4 in our FORMAT statement F10.4 indicates four decimal places.

7.04 FORMAT statements may specify more than one field. The number of fields desired is indicated by placing the required number in front of the letter specifying the mode.

Given the following example:

```
PRINT20,XLEN,WIDT,AREA
20 FORMAT(3F10.4)
```

a) The total number of fields provided in our FORMAT statement is _____.

b) The number of columns for the value of each of the Identifiers XLEN, WIDT, and AREA is _____.

- -

a) 3 b) 10

7.05 From studying the preceding frame, we can see that to specify more than one field of real mode, we must indicate the number of fields desired by placing a number in front of the letter F. (True or False)

- -

True

7.06 Assuming this program segment appears in our program:

```
PRINT20,SIDE,AREA
20 FORMAT(2F10.4)
```

the field specification that results is _____.

a) _ _ _ _ _ _ . _ _ _ _

b) _ _ _ _ _ _ . _ _ _ _ | _ _ _ _ _ _ . _ _ _ _

Choose either a or b.

- -

b

Note: The 2 in front of the F specifies two fields of 10 columns each with 4 decimal places. The vertical line separates the fields and will not appear in the actual output.

7.07 To have numbers printed as integers the letter I is used in the FORMAT statement.

Study this program segment:

```
      KARE=25.2
      PRINT30,KARE
   30 FORMAT(I10)
```

The above FORMAT statement would cause our output to be printed in _____ mode.

- -

integer Note the appearance of the output:

_ _ _ _ _ _ _ _ 2 5

Note: Truncation occurred when 25.2, a floating point number, was assigned to a fixed point Identifier, KARE. The number 25 was then printed in columns 9 and 10. The dashed lines indicate the print positions and will not actually appear in the computer output.

7.08 It is necessary at times to require two I fields for our output.

Study this program segment:

```
      KSID=2
      KARE=KSID*KSID
      PRINT60,KSID,KARE
   60 FORMAT(2I10)
```

The results would appear as _____.

a) _ _ _ _ _ _ _ _ _ 2 | _ _ _ _ _ _ _ _ _ 4

b) _ _ _ _ _ _ _ _ 2 4

Choose a or b.

- -

a 2I10 designates <u>two</u> fields of ten columns each.

7.09 Some programs may require printing values for several Identifiers. Study this program segment:

```
      LENG=5
      KWID=3
      KARE=LENG*KWID
      PRINT80,LENG,KWID,KARE
   80 FORMAT(3I10)
```

Enter the correct values in the print positions specified by the FORMAT statement.

```
_ _ _ _ _ _ _ _ _ _ | _ _ _ _ _ _ _ _ _ _ | _ _ _ _ _ _ _ _ _ _
```

- -

```
_ _ _ _ _ _ _ _ _ 5 | _ _ _ _ _ _ _ _ _ 3 | _ _ _ _ _ _ _ _ 1 5
```

THE INPUT FORMAT STATEMENT

The FORMAT statement is a specification statement. When used with a READ statement, it specifies the form of the data being read in and where this data may be found on the punched card.

The following discussion concerns itself with one specific FORMAT statement:

statement number FORMAT (F10.4)

The statement number is the statement number referenced in the READ statement. It is followed by the word FORMAT followed by a left parenthesis; the letter F, used to specify real mode; the number 10, specifying the total number of columns required for one item of data; a decimal point; the number 4, specifying the number of decimal places in the item of data, and a right parenthesis. (Same requirements as for output specification.)

Listed below is an example of a FORMAT statement used with a READ statement:

```
READ80,RADIUS
80 FORMAT(F10.4)
```

Note: As mentioned above, the F specifies that the computer is to look for a real number. The 10.4 specifies ten columns: one column for the sign (plus or minus), four columns for a whole number, one column for the decimal point, and four columns for the decimal places.

The input FORMAT statement specifies the number of card columns used to contain the number being read. This is called the field width. When a FORMAT statement specifies a field width for a card, the number to be read must not exceed the bounds of that field when punched.

7.10 The field width specified by the statement:

```
80 FORMAT(F10.4)
```

is _____ columns.

- -

10

7.11 Study this program segment:

```
READ80,RADI
80 FORMAT(F10.4)
```

The FORMAT statement is referenced in the READ statement by the statement number _____.

- -

80

7.12 In the preceding frame, the (F10.4) is an instruction to look for a real number in the first _____ columns of the card.

- -

10

7.13 In the following example:

```
READ70,SIDE
70 FORMAT(F10.4)
```

the statement number 70 in the READ statement tells the computer to refer to the statement numbered 70. The statement numbered 70 provides _____ columns for the number with which we are dealing.

- -

10

PREPARING DATA CARDS

Since many programs will require the use of data cards, it is important for even the beginning programmer to understand thoroughly the basic rules involved in preparing data. The data list must contain the values to be read in the same physical order as the Identifier(s) appear in the READ statement list.

Examples:

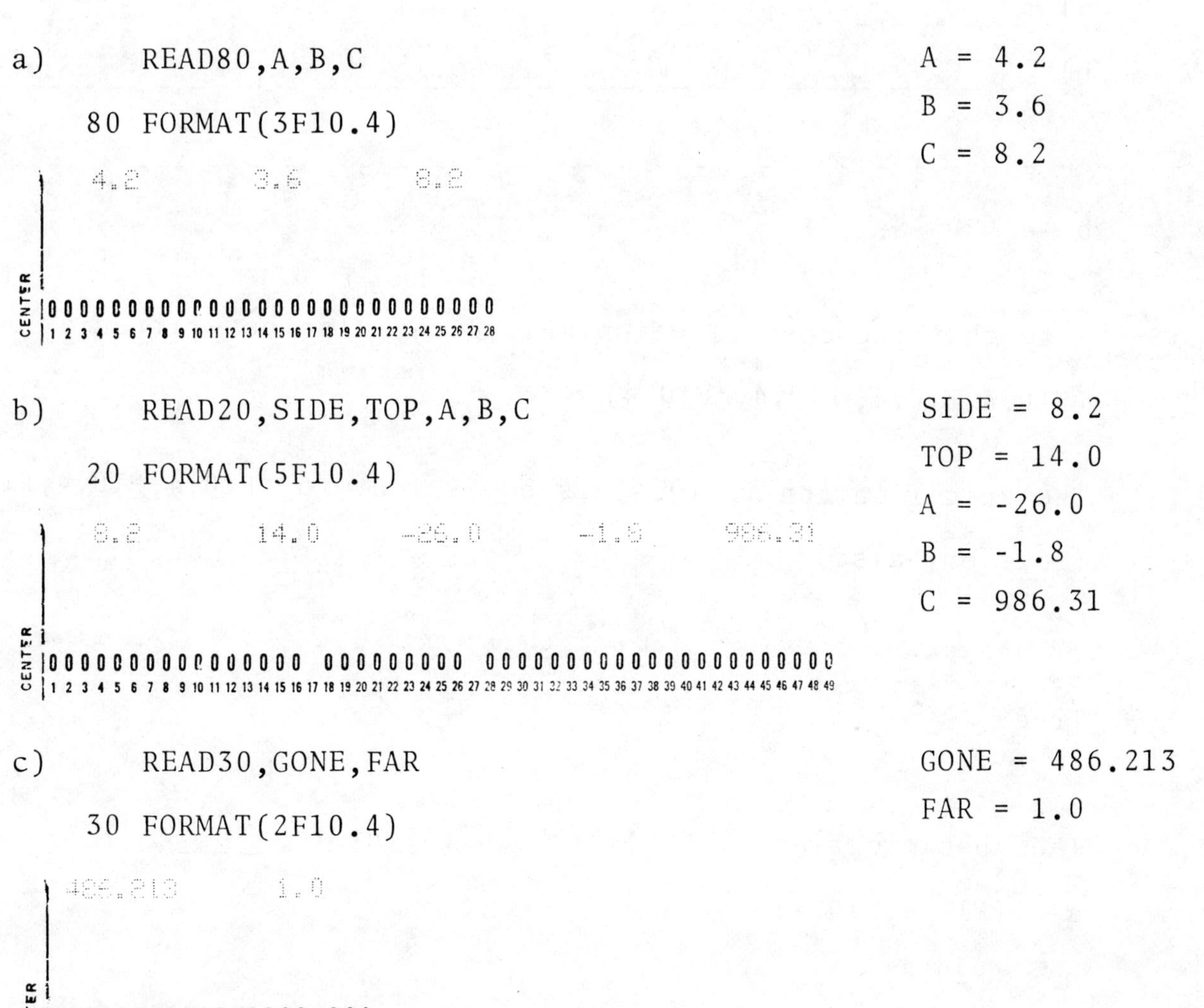

	FORTRAN Statement	Results Stored in Computer
a)	READ80,A,B,C 80 FORMAT(3F10.4)	A = 4.2 B = 3.6 C = 8.2
b)	READ20,SIDE,TOP,A,B,C 20 FORMAT(5F10.4)	SIDE = 8.2 TOP = 14.0 A = -26.0 B = -1.8 C = 986.31
c)	READ30,GONE,FAR 30 FORMAT(2F10.4)	GONE = 486.213 FAR = 1.0

7.14 Assume we wish the computer to read in more than one number. A specification of 10.4 can be used for each Identifier.

Study this program segment:

```
READ80,PRIN,RATE,TIME
80 FORMAT(3F10.4)
```

This FORMAT tells the computer to look for the Identifier values of PRIN, RATE, and TIME, in the first 30 columns on a card. Select the FORMAT provided above:

a) _ _ _ _ _ . _ _ _ _

b) _ _ _ _ _ . _ _ _ _ | _ _ _ _ _ . _ _ _ _ | _ _ _ _ _ . _ _ _ _

- -

b

7.15 Note that the specification 4F10.4 can also be written as (F10.4,F10.4, F10.4, F10.4).

The specification (3F10.4) is equivalent to (F10.4,F10.4,F10.4). (True or False)

- -

True

7.16 The specification (2F10.4) is equivalent to _____.

a) (F10.4,F10.4)

b) (F20.8)

- -

a) (F10.4,F10.4)

Note: A real data value may be placed anywhere in the field but it must be completely contained within the field.

7.17 The following FORMAT would accommodate the numbers 20.3, 14.8, and 1.76:

```
      READ20,G,T,X
   20 FORMAT(3F10.4)
```

(True or False)

- -

True

_ _ _ 2 0 . 3 0 0 0 | _ _ _ 1 4 . 8 0 0 0 | _ _ _ _ 1 . 7 6 0 0

There are cases when an I field FORMAT is desired. An I field is desired when integers are to be read into the program. When reading an I field, the numbers must be "right justified", or positioned to the extreme right of the field. Failure to do so may result in the computer providing zeroes in blank columns to the right of the numbers.

Study this program segment:

```
      READ30,JADE
   30 FORMAT(I10)
```

This instruction would cause the computer to look in the first ten columns of a card for the value of the Identifier JADE.

7.18 Assuming the data to be read is 675, select the card that is correctly punched. _____

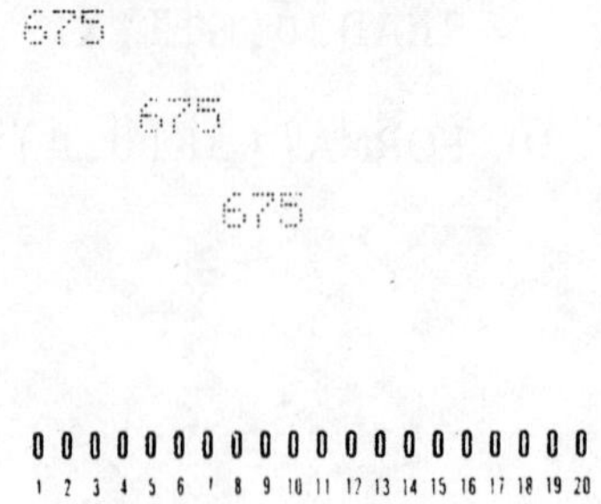

675

675

675

0 0 0 0 0 0 0 0 0 0 0 0 0 0 0 0 0 0 0 0
1 2 3 4 5 6 7 8 9 10 11 12 13 14 15 16 17 18 19 20

- -

c a) would require that 6750000000 be assigned to JADE.

b) would require that 675000 be assigned to JADE.

7.19 An input FORMAT statement may specify input of more than one number of integer mode.

The following statements:

```
READ7,J,K,L
7 FORMAT(3I10)
```

would direct the computer to read _____ numbers of integer mode.

- -

3

7.20 Given the following program segment:

```
READ40,NUMB,LIST
40 FORMAT(2I10)
```

the computer would look for the value of the two Identifiers in the first _____ columns of a card.

The largest number of digits either Identifier may have is _____.

- -

20 10 if positive
9 if negative

7.21 FORMAT(2I10) is equivalent to FORMAT(I10,I10). (True or False)

- -

True

7.22 Study this program segment:

```
READ50,L
50 FORMAT(I10)
```

This would be correct formatting for the number 5280. (True or False)

- -

True The number is positive and does not exceed ten digits.

7.23 A READ statement that uses an integer Identifier must be provided with integer values.

The Identifier that requires an integer FORMAT is _____

a) ZEBRA b) PILL c) NUM

- -

c) NUM

7.24 In a READ statement, the Identifiers may be in either mode, provided that the data list is in the same order, and that the FORMAT statement provides the correct mode.

In the following example:

```
      READ60,NUMBER,TABLE
   60 FORMAT(I10,F10.4)
```

the values on the card would be assigned in the order in which they occur.

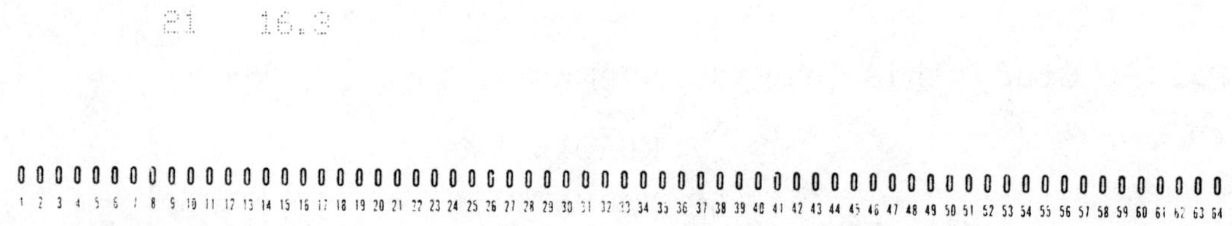

```
      21    16.3

0000000000000000000000000000000000000000000000000000000000000000
1 2 3 4 5 6 7 8 9 10 11 12 13 14 15 16 17 18 19 20 21 22 23 24 25 26 27 28 29 30 31 32 33 34 35 36 37 38 39 40 41 42 43 44 45 46 47 48 49 50 51 52 53 54 55 56 57 58 59 60 61 62 63 64
```

(a) The number assigned to the Identifier NUMBER would be _____.

(b) The number assigned to the Identifier TABLE would be _____.

- -

(a) 21 (b) 16.3

The list in the READ or PRINT statement may contain both real and integer Identifiers.

Example:

```
READ40, A,B,C,L,M
```

C ← FOR COMMENT | STATEMENT NUMBER | CONTINUATION | FORTRAN STATEMENT

Since both modes appear in the READ list, assume the data to be:

```
3.0        2.16        5.02        7111        68
```

then

A is assigned a value of 3.0
B is assigned a value of 2.16
C is assigned a value of 5.02
L is assigned a value of 7111
M is assigned a value of 68

7.25 Write the input FORMAT statement required in the previous frame.

- -

```
40 FORMAT(3F10.4,2I10)
```

All our examples of FORMAT statements thus far have been confined to only two FORMAT specifications.

1. Real: F10.4
2. Integer: I10

Before beginning a detailed explanation of some of the many other possible formatting specifications, a few general ideas should be presented.

1. Each input or output statement may have an associated FORMAT statement; however, it is not necessary to have separate FORMAT statements for each input or output statement in a program. The same FORMAT statement could be used for more than one input or output, or for both input and output.
2. FORMAT statements in our programs have followed immediately after the associated input or output. Actually, since FORMAT statements are non-executable statements, they may be placed anywhere in the program as long as one is not the last statement of a DO, and as long as they come before the END statement.
3. The specification provided must be large enough to accommodate the number. If the specification is too large, the unused columns are merely left blank; however, if the specification is too small and cannot accommodate the number, an error will result.
4. A sufficient number of specifications must be provided. If more specifications are provided than are needed, the reading or printing will merely stop when the list is processed. For instance, if five specifications are provided but only three Identifiers are involved, the values for the three Identifiers will appear and the remaining specification will be unused. However, if five Identifiers are to be read and only three specifications are provided in the FORMAT statement, the first three Identifier values will be read from one data card and the last two Identifier values will be read from a second data card using the first two specifications in the FORMAT. The same error in an output FORMAT would result in three values printed on one line and two on the next line.

5. If a real Identifier is listed in the READ or PRINT, a real specification must be provided in the FORMAT statement. If an integer Identifier is listed in the READ or PRINT, an integer specification must be provided in the FORMAT statement.

F SPECIFICATIONS

The general form for a real FORMAT specification is

nFw.d

An explanation of each character follows:

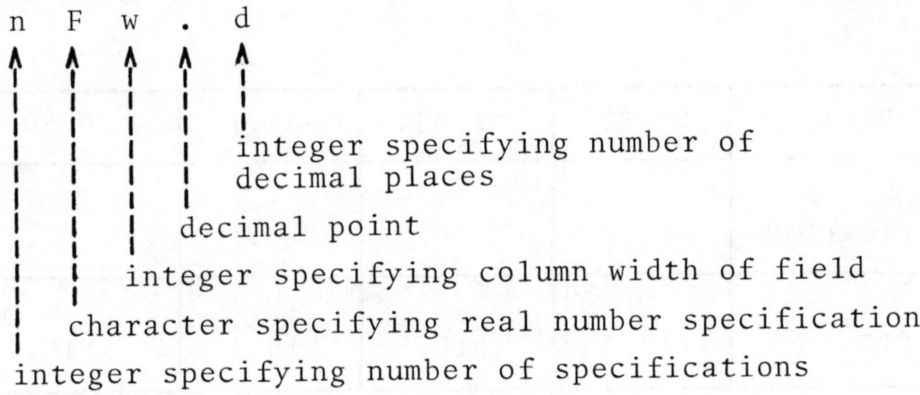

If only one field is required, it is not necessary to show the 1 in front of the F.

The preceding FORMAT specification describes the layout for a single or multiple input or output field.

Each time a real input or output FORMAT specification is constructed, care must be taken to provide enough columns to accommodate:

1. the desired number of digits
2. a decimal point
3. an algebraic sign for negative numbers

It is usually allowable to provide a FORMAT specification larger than required since no error will result. On the other hand, a specification providing fewer columns than needed will introduce an error, or truncation.

Analyze the examples which show the required specifications for input values.

INPUT DATA	14.32	+2.034	-44.1	+.00597	-9.86
MINIMUM SPECIFICATION	F5.2	F6.3	F5.1	F7.5	F5.2
SAFE SPECIFICATION	F10.2	F10.3	F10.1	F10.5	F10.2

Now let us examine these output specifications and the printed output.

NUMBER IN STORAGE	FIELD WIDTH SPECIFICATION	PRINTED OUTPUT	COMMENT
77.784	F6.2	∧77.78	the 4 is omitted
156.9	F8.3	∧156.900	two zeros are added
-65.333	F10.3	∧∧∧-65.333	
97.68	F5.2	97.68	
.009	F7.4	∧0.0090	
156.9	F5.2	error message or *****	

When writing FORMAT statements to be used with output statements, particular care must be taken to provide a FORMAT that will not result in a character being printed in the first column of the line.

I SPECIFICATIONS

The general form for an integer FORMAT specification is:

nIw

Each character is explained in the diagram below.

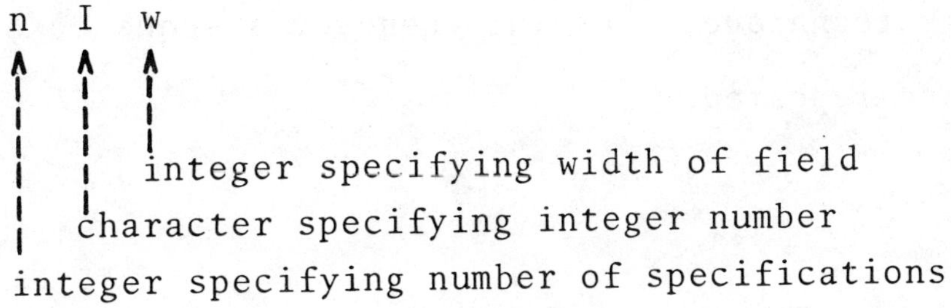

```
n  I  w
^  ^  ^
|  |  |
|  |  integer specifying width of field
|  character specifying integer number
integer specifying number of specifications
```

The preceding specification prescribes the layout for single or multiple input or output fields. Since the numbers involved are integers, the programmer need concern himself only with the number of digits in the whole number and any possible negative signs when providing the minimum number of columns in the field.

Listed below are examples of integer mode FORMAT specifications.

a)
```
      READ20,L                                Data
   20 FORMAT(I4)                              6250
```

b)
```
      READ20,I,J                              Data
   20 FORMAT(2I5)                             -5000ΛΛ675
```

Note: The number must be right justified within the field.

When both integer and real Identifiers occur in the same list of a READ or PRINT statement, the accompanying FORMAT statement must provide the correct fields.

```
      READ20,X,J,Y,K
   20 FORMAT(F10.4,I5,F10.4,I5)
```

The above FORMAT could also be written in a short-hand form through the use of parentheses.

```
   20 FORMAT(2(F10.4,I5))
```

This technique is useful whenever a sequence of specifications is to be repeated.

X SPECIFICATIONS

A third type of specification that is provided in FORMAT statements in FORTRAN is the blank specification. There are many situations where the programmer wishes to provide blank spaces for ease of punching the input or ease of reading the output. In other cases, the programmer may wish to have the computer ignore data or information previously punched on a card - such as customers names. Finally, the programmer can insure against accidentally printing a number in the first column of the output line by specifying a blank. The blank field can be provided by means of the X specification.

The form of the X specification is:

nX

When used for output, the number preceding the X specifies the number of columns to be left blank. Thus:

```
FORMAT(6X,I5,4X,F10.4)
```

would direct the computer to leave the first six columns blank, provide five columns for a integer value, leave four columns blank, and then provide ten columns for a real value. This improves the legibility of the output sheet and allows the programmer to line up his columns of numbers with alphabetic headings.

When used with input, the X specification directs the computer to ignore certain card columns. In this way, data that already exists on the card and is not pertinent to the program can be ignored.

Strange things can happen if care is not taken to avoid providing an undesired character in column one of the print image.

```
FORMAT (I2)
```

The above FORMAT looks harmless enough. However, if the value to be printed is 10, the character provided for column one would be a 1. The 1 would direct the computer to skip to a new page and only a zero would be printed on the second page.

For this reason, it is advisable to deliberately provide for a blank in the first column of the output image.

```
FORMAT (6X,5F10.4)
```

The 6X provides for six blanks in the beginning of the line and eliminates the possibility of accidentally providing an undesired character in the print image.

H SPECIFICATIONS

A fourth type of specification that is available to the programmer in FORTRAN is the Hollerith field. Its function is to make the output more easily understood by the reader.

The Hollerith specification directs the computer to print out specified alphabetic characters or symbols. In the F and I specifications, the computer printed out the current numerical values for specified Identifiers; in the H-specification, alphabetic characters themselves are printed out.

The FORMAT for the Hollerith specification consists of a number followed by an H. The H informs the computer that it is to print out alphabetic characters and symbols.

The number preceding the H informs the computer that a number of spaces will be required for the alphabetic characters and symbols. A Hollerith field may be any length desired as long as it does not exceed the allowable print line size.

It is absolutely necessary that the number in the Hollerith specification be exactly correct. One space too many or too few will probably result in an error message and the program being rejected, and will at least result in incorrect output. Therefore, since this count is so critical, we should consider exactly what should be counted.

Let us assume that we wish to print out, "The roots are imaginary". The PRINT and corresponding FORMAT statement with the Hollerith specification would be:

```
        PRINT40
     40 FORMAT(24H THE ROOTS ARE IMAGINARY)
```

Notice that no Identifiers are required in the PRINT statement. There are twenty alphabetic characters that we want printed out. There are also four blank spaces. The parenthesis will not be printed out, and is not counted. Each blank and each character after the 24H is counted. If we wanted to end our sentence with a period, the period would have to be shown, and the count would have to go up to 25. With our statement as it is written, using a 23H or a 25H could cause an error message to appear.

The H specification can be used in the same FORMAT statement with an F, I, or X specification. Let us consider the following FORMAT statement.

```
        PRINT2,A,ROOT
      2 FORMAT(6X,19HTHE SQUARE ROOT OF ,F10.4,8H IS +/- ,F10.4)
```

Here the H specification is used with an X and two F specifications. The 6X provides for blanks in the first six columns of our output. The 19H specifies that 19 spaces will be required, and that the computer is to print out THE SQUARE ROOT OF . There are fifteen alphabetic characters and four blank spaces. Note that there is no blank provided between 19H and the first word to be printed, but that there is a blank space provided at the end of the printing.

The comma following the blank space is not counted because this comma merely separates the specifications and is not to be printed. The Hollerith specification is followed by an F specification providing a ten-column field in which to print the current value of A. This is followed by another H specification and then an F specification in which the current value of ROOT is printed. If A=6.25 and ROOT=2.5 the output will appear as follows:

```
∧∧∧∧∧∧THE∧SQUARE∧ROOT∧OF∧∧∧∧∧6.2500∧IS∧+/-∧∧∧∧∧2.5000
```

Many versions of FORTRAN have an option available to the programmer which makes the Hollerith specification easier to use. Instead of counting the characters and using the H, the series of characters may be simply enclosed in quotes as follows, that is

```
2 FORMAT(6X,19HTHE SQUARE ROOT OF ,F10.4,8H IS +/- ,F10.4)
```

could be replaced by

```
2 FORMAT (6X,'THE SQUARE ROOT OF ',F10.4,' IS +/- ',F10.4)
```

This option may or may not be available and the reader is advised to check before using this feature.

E SPECIFICATIONS

The use of the F specification with real numbers has been discussed. However, the F specification has disadvantages that have not been emphasized. If the numbers being processed are too large for the specification, the program will be rejected. Since the programmer does not always know exactly how large or how small the numbers may become, this can be a serious disadvantage. FORTRAN has another type specification that is commonly used with real numbers when the programmer cannot predict with certainty how large or how small the numbers may become, and that is the E specification, written in a form that parallels what is called scientific notation in mathematics. In scientific notation, the number 756 would be written as $7.56 \times 10^{+2}$; in E form it could be written as 7.56E+02.

The number .00756 could be 7.56E-03. The form for the E value consists of a real number followed by an E, a plus or a minus sign, and a two digit number. The plus sign and the two digit number describe the number of places to the right the decimal must be moved to convert to a real number as normally written. A minus sign and the two digit number describe the number of places the decimal must be moved to the left to convert to a real number as normally written.

Example: 7.56E+02 = 756

7.56E-03 = .00756

In E notation, the number may be expressed as any number plus or minus the correct value.

Example: 756 = 7.56E+02 = 75600E-02

.00756 = 7.56E-03 = 756E-05 = .0000756E+02

The advantage of working with numbers in the E specification is that the width of the field is independent of the size of that number. It is dependent only on the degree of accuracy to which the number is to be reported.

The E type specification is of the form:

```
E w . d
↑ ↑ ↑ ↑
| | | number of decimal places
| | decimal point
| field width
indicates E type
```

The w designates an integer that specifies the complete width of the field. It must provide for:

1. A column for the algebraic sign of the number.
2. At least one column for one digit to the left of the decimal point.
3. A column for the decimal point.
4. The number of columns required for the desired number of decimal places.
5. Four columns for the full form of the exponent: namely, the E, the sign and a two digit integer exponent.

Thus the input quantities below required the specifications shown:

Input	5.43E+04	258.56E+02
Specification	E8.2	E10.2

Input	-12.E-05	95.E-05
Specification	E8.0	E7.0

An output quantity 350.7 would be printed as shown depending on the specification shown:

```
E11.0      ΛΛΛΛΛ0.E+03
E11.2      ΛΛΛ0.35E+03
E11.3      ΛΛ0.351E+03
E11.4      Λ0.3507E+03
```

Notice that with the last specification the number utilizes the entire field width if it is a negative number, and all but the first column if it is positive. This means that if you have two E fields in your FORMAT, there will be little or no space between the numbers unless blank spaces are provided.

A SPECIFICATIONS

The H specification allows the printing of a sequence of alphameric characters. With A specifications, we can read and print alphameric characters. Alphameric characters include letters, numbers and certain other characters.

In some cases, it is helpful to work with alphameric characters. This may seem surprising at first, since we have not heretofore mentioned operating with alphabetic characters in the same way in which we operate with numberic characters. However, the programmer may want to move this data from one place to another in storage or to perform operations upon the data - perhaps for the purpose of sorting it in alphabetic order.

When alphameric data is to be processed in the program, the A specification is used to read it into the computer and to print it. Reading alphameric information under the A specification allows the programmer to assign this information to an Identifier; then it may be treated as any other Identifier. The Identifier assigned by the programmer may be either that of an integer Identifier or a real Identifier. However, if the Identifier is to be used in an arithmetic or logical expression, the name assigned must conform to the mode of the expression.

The general form of the A specification is:

```
n A w
↑ ↑ ↑
| | designates an integer specifying the number
| | of characters to be processed
| |
| indicates A type
|
designates an integer specifying the number of
times the specification is to be repeated
```

Assume that we have a data card containing the letter X in the first column. Input statements to read and assign X to the Identifier SPY are:

```
   READ20,SPY
20 FORMAT(A1)
```

If a card contained the characters JOB1 in the first four columns, the statements which would direct the computer to read JOB1 and assign the value to the Identifier SHIP are:

```
   READ30,SHIP
30 FORMAT(A4)
```

DATA STATEMENTS

The DATA statement is a non-executable specification statement. Its function is to assign initial values - integer, real, or alphameric - to Identifiers. The advantage of using a DATA statement to set up constants rather than writing the constants directly in the statements of the program is that fewer machine language instructions are required. It is also much less cumbersome than preparing the values on an input medium and reading them in as is necessary with alphameric quantities.

The general form of the DATA statement is:

DATA list/a_1,a_2.....a_n/list/b_1,b_2.....b_n/.....

For list, the programmer substitutes a list of Identifiers separated by commas. For a_1,a_2.....a_n the programmer substitutes the initial values separated by commas which are to be assigned to each of the Identifiers in the associated list. There must be a correspondence between the initial values and the Identifiers in the list, because the value of a_1 is assigned to the first Identifier in the list, the value of a_2 is assigned to the second Identifier, and so on. The values substituted may be integer, real, or alphameric.

Examples:

DATA X/5.6/

5.6 is assigned to X

DATA X,C,I/4.3,0.53E-05,9/

4.3 is assigned to X

0.53×10^{-5} is assigned to C

9 is assigned to I

DATA A,B/6.9,3.14/AB1,AB2/7.3,5.9/

6.9 is assigned to A

3.14 is assigned to B

7.3 is assigned to AB1

5.9 is assigned to AB2

Identifiers defined initially by means of a DATA statement may be redefined in the same manner as any other Identifier in the course of the execution of the program. Normally, however, they are not redefined, but are used as constant values. If the Identifiers initialized in a DATA statement are redefined in the program, they cannot be re-initialized by transferring control to the DATA statement: an Assignment statement must be used to redefine these Identifiers.

MULTIPLE RECORD FORMATS

The illustrative programs presented thus far have all assumed that all the data cards used in any one program will have the same FORMAT. Actually, the programmer is usually faced with processing data cards with varying FORMATS. In FORTRAN, the symbol / (slash) is employed to handle this situation.

The slash is used to indicate a skip to a new card or line in FORMAT statements. If a first card to be read has six integer values, and the second card has eight real values, the FORMAT statement might be:

```
FORMAT (6I10,/,8F9.2)
```

With this FORMAT, the first, third, fifth, etc., cards would have six integer values and the second, fourth, sixth, etc., cards would have eight real values.

A very common situation consists of one card of one FORMAT specification followed by several cards of second FORMAT specification. The computer can be directed to read these cards by the use of parentheses enclosing the second specification.

```
FORMAT (6I10,/,(8F9.2))
```

This would direct the computer to read one card with six integer values and then to read a series of cards, each containing eight real values, until the read list was exhausted.

CARRIAGE CONTROL

The attached printing device for most computer systems does not actually print the first character in the output image. Instead, the character is interpreted by the printing device as a "carriage control" character which causes the printer to space down the page in various ways.

In many computers, the following characters appearing in column one of an output FORMAT statement will cause the indicated carriage control operation to occur:

b (blank)	Normal (single) space
0 (zero)	Double space
1 (one)	Skips to a new page
+ (plus)	Does not space (prints on same line as before)

GENERAL READ AND WRITE STATEMENTS

The input/output statements presented earlier in this chapter are the forms used in WATFOR/WATFIV. The general form of input/output for FORTRAN is

```
READ(DN,FN)list
WRITE(DN,FN)list
```

where DN refers to a device number and FN refers to a FORMAT statement number.

e.g.

```
READ(5,22)SIDE
WRITE(6,24)SIDE,AREA
```

The device numbers 5 and 6 are unique to an installation and the reader should check before attempting to use this form.

As this form is quite commonly used in FORTRAN programs, in the remainder of this text we will use this general input/output form.

CONTINUATION CARDS

It has been pointed out that columns 1 through 5 on the Hollerith card are used for statement numbers and columns 7 to 72 are used for FORTRAN statements. However, the use of column 6 has not been discussed. Column 6 is reserved for the situation when a statement is too long to be contained in columns 7 to 72 on one card. In this case, the statement may be continued in columns 7 to 72 of a second card and a third. However, the computer must be informed that the statement is being continued on the second card, or it will read the second card as though it contained a second separate and distinct statement. The method for informing the computer that the second card is a continuation card is to punch a digit in column 6 of the second card. The first card is left blank in column 6, the second card has a 1 in column 6, the third card would have the digit 2 punched in column 6, etc. The number of continuation cards permissible varies depending on the particular version of FORTRAN.

TYPE DECLARATIONS

The value assigned to an Identifier is an integer or a real as designated by the first letter of the Identifier. As explained previously, Identifiers beginning with I, J, K, L, M, or N are integer Identifiers, whereas Identifiers beginning with any other letter are real Identifiers. This is a predefined or implicit data type specification. However, the data type specification for integer or real Identifiers may be either implicit or explicit.

An explicit type specification is accomplished by listing an Identifier in a Type Declaration statement. By use of a Type Declaration statement, the value assigned to any Identifier (regardless of its first letter) may be designated as real or integer. The general forms of the Type Declaration statements are:

```
INTEGER a,b,c.....
REAL a,b,c.....
```

The programmer substitutes for a,b,c..... a list of Identifiers separated by commas. The list may include:

1. Identifiers
2. Identifiers for arrays (see Array chapter)
3. Subprogram Identifiers for Assignment statement functions or FUNCTION subprograms (see Subprogram chapter)

Examples of Type Declaration statements:

```
INTEGER I,XRAY,S,JOB
REAL K,INT,PRIN,BAL
```

The following rules govern Type Declaration statements:

1. Both predefined, or implicit type specification, and Type Declaration statements may be used in the same program.
2. INTEGER specifies that all the Identifiers listed in the statement are integer type.
3. REAL specifies that all the Identifiers listed in the statement are real type.
4. The appearance of an Identifier in a Type Declaration statement nullifies the predefined type indicated by the first letter of the Identifier.
5. Type Declaration statements are placed first in the source program.
6. The appearance of a name in a Type Declaration statement list designates the type permanently in that program. Once established, it is impossible to change the type.
7. An Identifier may appear in only one Type Declaration statement in a program.
8. An Identifier designated to be of a particular type may be assigned only values of the type specified.

COMMENT CARDS

It is often desirable to introduce statements and have them reproduced as part of the program listing, but not have them processed as part of the program. For instance, the programmer may want to head the listing of his program with his name and the title of his program. This can be done by means of a comment card. Any card may be designated a comment card merely by punching a C in column 1. Any statement then punched in columns 2 to 80 on that card will be printed, but will not be processed as part of the program. If a comment extends to a second card, a C must be punched in column 1 of the second card also. Comment cards may be placed anywhere in the program except within a set of continuation cards, and the comments will appear in the program listing in the same relative position. The use of comment cards is illustrated in several sample programs.

CHAPTER EIGHT

ARRAYS AND THE DIMENSION STATEMENT

ARRAY NOTATION

In previous discussion, Identifiers such as A, B, C, etc., have been employed to represent values in the data list.

e.g. READ(5,38)A,B,C

data list 6.0 8.2 3.9

To distinguish individual members of the data list, a new Identifier has been chosen for each value.

In many instances, it is very convenient to represent an entire data list, or array of values, by a single Identifier. When an Identifier represents an array, the members of the array (called elements) are distinguished from one another by means of a number called a subscript. The subscript is written within parentheses following the Identifier.

```
A(5)          A(I)            B(N+1)
DIFF(I)       ARRAY(INDEX)    NAME(2*K+9)
```

All of the above are examples of Identifiers with subscripts.

In FORTRAN, the subscripted Identifier may be in either integer or real mode, but the subscript itself must be an integer.

The subscript itself is also limited in the types of expressions that are permitted.

Legal Subscript Expression	Example
Constant	(3)
Identifier	(J)
Identifier plus or minus a constant	(I+2) or (I-3)
Constant multiplied by an Identifier	(4*J) or (-6*L)
Constant multiplied by an Identifier plus or minus a constant	(4*J+6) or (8*K-2)

The subscript indicates which element of the array is being referenced. For example, A(5) indicates the fifth element of the array A. A(I) indicates the "Ith" element, and represents any element of the array A, depending on the current value of I. If the value of N is 9, then the subscript expression N+1, in B(N+1), will indicate the 10th element of the array B. This method of naming the elements of an array is quite similar to the way in which names are given to a family of persons. Each member of a family has the same last name, and is distinguished from the other members by a unique first name.

The use of the subscripted Identifier provides a very efficient technique for reading a list - the self-indexing technique. In this type of input statement list, the Identifier with its subscript is followed by an index definition exactly like the one used in a DO statement. For instance:

```
READ (5,20) (S(I),I=1,100)
```

This statement will direct the computer to perform the same operations as it would perform if directed to:

```
READ (5,20) S(1), S(2), S(3),..,S(100)
```

In other words, the statement directs the computer to read one hundred values of S, store each value in the computer as the value for S(1), S(2), etc., where it can be referred to later in the program merely by specifying S(1), S(2), etc.

INPUT FOR AN ARRAY

Consider the following data list of 100 values punched ten numbers to the card in seven column fields.

```
3.4  6.0 7.2 8.3 9.0 1.6 18.4 9.5 2.5 3.0
8.2 93.6 ... ... ... ...  ... ... ... ...
...  ... ... ... ... ...  ... ... ... ...
...  ... ... ... ... ...  ... ... ... ...
...  ... ... ... ... ...  ... ... ... ...
...  ... ... ... ... ...  ... ... ... ...
...  ... ... ... ... ...  ... ... ......
...  ... ... ... ... ...  ... ... ... ...
...  ... ... ... ... ...  ... ... ... ...
...  ... ... ... ... ...  ... ... ... 5.7
```

This data list may be assigned to the array S by a READ and FORMAT statement as follows:

```
       .....
       READ(5,30) (S(I),I=1,100)
    30 FORMAT (10F7.2)
```

Note: A DIMENSION statement indicating the Identifier S is to represent an array would have to precede these statements. This will be discussed later in this chapter.

The effect of either preceding program segment is as follows:

```
S(1)=3.4
S(2)=6.0
S(3)=7.2
S(4)=8.3
.....
S(10)=3.0
S(11)=8.2
.....
.....
S(100)=5.7
```

Note: A value in the data list should not be confused with the subscript in the Identifier to which the value is assigned.

The index definition as used in input lists may have Identifiers for lower or upper limits, and may use the optional third quantity defining an increment other than one. For instance:

```
READ (5,30) (S(I),I=1,N,3)
```

is perfectly legal.

Like most other FORTRAN statements, the form which you must observe is exact. The subscripted Identifier must be separated from the index definition by a comma and the entire sequence - Identifiers, subscripts, and index definitions must be enclosed in parentheses.

OPERATIONS ON ELEMENTS OF AN ARRAY

Any legal FORTRAN operation may be performed on the elements of an array.

Example:

```
W=S(1)+S(2)
X=S(1)*2.5
Y=S(1)*S(10)*S(100)
Z=S(2)**2
```

are all legal FORTRAN Assignment statements.

If the four Assignment statements above were executed with the values of the array S given above, the effect would be

```
W=3.4+6.0
X=3.4*2.5
Y=3.4*3.0*5.7
Z=6.0**2
```

SUM OF THE ELEMENTS OF AN ARRAY

The following program segment may be used to find the sum of the elements of an array S of 100 values:

```
   .....
   SUM=0
   DO 40 I=1,100
   SUM=SUM+S(I)
40 CONTINUE
   .....
```

OUTPUT FOR AN ARRAY

Either of the following program segments may be used to output an array of 100 values in a column.

1)
```
      .....
      DO 72 I=1,100
      WRITE(6,49) A(I)
   49 FORMAT(6X,F10.4)
   72 CONTINUE
```

2)
```
      WRITE(6,49)(A(I),I=1,100)
   49 FORMAT(6X,F10.4)
```

Both methods could either output the entire array or any portion desired with modification of the DO or implied DO parameters.

The number of values on each line of output may be varied by appropriate changes in the FORMAT statement of method 2.

THE DIMENSION STATEMENT

When a subscripted Identifier is used in FORTRAN, a DIMENSION statement must also be used. The DIMENSION statement specifies the size of any list or array of the subscripted Identifier. It consists of the word DIMENSION followed by the name of the Identifier and a number enclosed in parentheses specifying the maximum number of values in the array.

The DIMENSION statement must appear in the program before any statement using the Identifier, and in no case should a subscript be allowed to exceed the size specified in the DIMENSION statement.

In our example, the DIMENSION statement would be

DIMENSION S(100)

At this point, it is worthwhile to consider a complete program which utilizes the following:

1. DIMENSION statement;
2. Input with subscripted Identifiers - using the self-indexing technique;
3. Operations upon subscripted Identifiers;
4. Output with subscripted Identifiers.

This program reads twenty scores from Hollerith cards containing ten scores per card, adds the scores, and then prints out the scores and the final sum in a single column.

The following pages contain the flow chart, and coding of this program.

Flow chart:

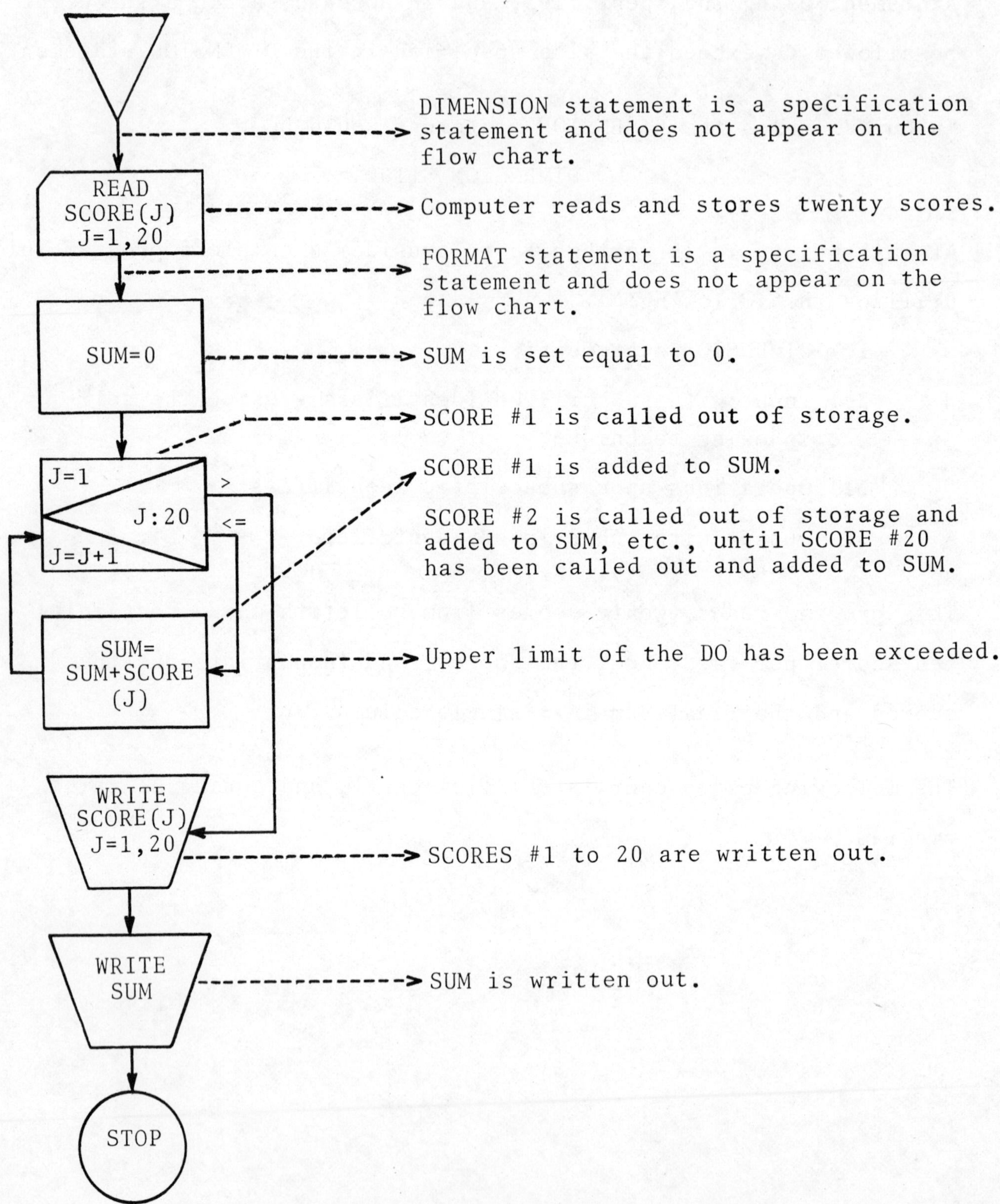

READ SCORE(J) J=1,20
SUM=0
J=1
J:20
J=J+1
>
<=
SUM= SUM+SCORE (J)
WRITE SCORE(J) J=1,20
WRITE SUM
STOP
DIMENSION statement is a specification statement and does not appear on the flow chart.
Computer reads and stores twenty scores.
FORMAT statement is a specification statement and does not appear on the flow chart.
SUM is set equal to 0.
SCORE #1 is called out of storage.
SCORE #1 is added to SUM.
SCORE #2 is called out of storage and added to SUM, etc., until SCORE #20 has been called out and added to SUM.
Upper limit of the DO has been exceeded.
SCORES #1 to 20 are written out.
SUM is written out.

Coding:

```
      DIMENSION SCORE(20)
      READ(5,62)(SCORE(J),J=1,20)
   62 FORMAT(10F7.2)
      SUM=0
      DO 29 J=1,20
   29 SUM=SUM+SCORE(J)
      WRITE(6,64)(SCORE(J),J=1,20)
   64 FORMAT(F7.2)
      WRITE(6,65)SUM
   65 FORMAT(6X,F10.2)
      STOP
      END
```

Note: The output would appear as a column of values.

When a program uses more than one array, a separate DIMENSION statement may be written for each subscripted Identifier, or all of the Identifiers may be listed in a single DIMENSION statement. Assume the program calls for the A array, the B array and the C array. Either of the following is permissible:

```
DIMENSION A(100)          DIMENSION A(100),B(100),C(100)
DIMENSION B(100)
DIMENSION C(100)
```

The reader is urged to study the following example of a program using the DIMENSION statement in a program requiring the use of more than one array.

Example:

There are 200 values in a data list. (Ten values per card in F7.2 fields.) The first 100 elements are to be considered the A array; the second 100 elements in the B array. All are real numbers. We wish to read in both arrays, and add the first element in the A array to the first element in the B array, then add the second element in A array to the second element in the B array, etc., and store the results in the C array. As output, we would like to display all three arrays.

Flow chart:

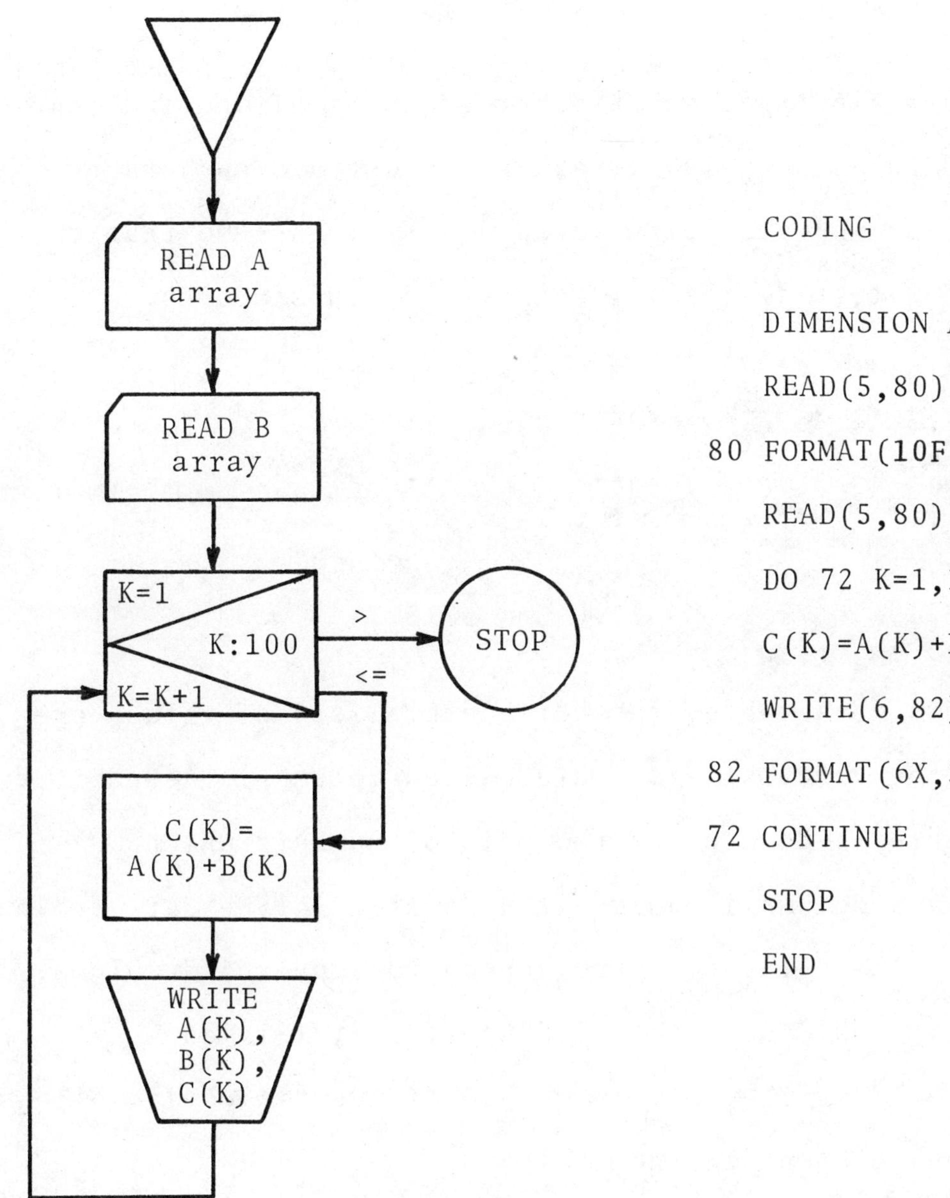

CODING

```
   DIMENSION A(100),B(100),C(100)
   READ(5,80)(A(I),I=1,100)
80 FORMAT(10F7.2)
   READ(5,80)(B(I),I=1,100)
   DO 72 K=1,100
   C(K)=A(K)+B(K)
   WRITE(6,82)A(K),B(K),C(K)
82 FORMAT(6X,3F10.2)
72 CONTINUE
   STOP
   END
```

ARRAYS WITH MORE THAN ONE SUBSCRIPT

The discussion of arrays presented thus far has involved arrays with only one subscript. These arrays are called vectors.

In working with certain types of data, programmers often find that considering the data as a table of values has certain advantages. The data table which appears below is an example. Assume that the table contains four test scores for each of thirty students.

```
98.6    75.2    83.6    95.0
75.3    69.7    85.8    64.3
....    ....    ....    ....
....    ....    ....    ....
....    ....    ....    ....
83.4    75.2    72.0    97.3
```

When working with a data table, the horizontal lists of values are called rows, and the vertical lists are called columns. A specific element of the table is denoted by the pair of numbers which indicate the row and column in which it appears. In the data table given above, the value 85.8 is in the second row and third column. Hence, this element could be identified as T(2,3); T is an arbitrarily chosen Identifier. This method of identification allows us to reference any element in the table.

In order to input a table of this form using subscripted Identifiers, a DIMENSION statement is required. Since the table consists of 30 rows and 4 columns, and T is the Identifier, the DIMENSION statement is

```
DIMENSION T(30,4)
```

The Identifier T is called a doubly subscripted Identifier. An array with two subscripts is also commonly called a matrix. The first subscript denotes the row, and the second subscript denotes the column. The two subscripts must be separated by a comma and enclosed within parentheses. The above DIMENSION statement, in effect, reserves a place for a 30 by 4 matrix.

The following sequence of statements will input the entire matrix:

```
      .....
      DIMENSION T(30,4)
      READ(5,40)((T(K,L),L=1,4),K=1,30)
   40 FORMAT(4F10.4)
      .....
```

The effect of the previous program segment is

```
T(1,1) = 98.6
T(1,2) = 75.2
T(1,3) = 83.6
T(1,4) = 95.0
T(2,1) = 75.3
.....
T(2,4) = 64.3
.....
.....
.....
T(30,3) = 72.0
T(30,4) = 97.3
```

READ(5,40)((T(K,L),L=1,4),K=1,30) instructs the computer to read 120 numbers into an array in the following order:

T(1,1),T(1,2),T(1,3).....T(25,1),T(25,2),T(25,3).....T(30,4)

The first four numbers will be read as the first row, the second four as the second row, etc. The subscript L advances initially: when it reaches its limit, the subscript K is advanced.

When using self-indexing statements with double subscripts, care must be taken to follow the exact format. If any part of the form is missing, the computer will reject the program with an error message.

The use of the double subscript is demonstrated in Sample Program 10 in APPENDIX III.

VARIATIONS IN THE USE OF ARRAYS

In our initial discussion of input, we mentioned one method of providing input was with the use of the self generating DO loop. This, in effect, generates internally the data requested. Since the reader is now familiar with the DO statement and arrays, it may be of interest to indicate the possibility of generating a vector without the necessity of providing data.

Example:

```
      DIMENSION A(100)
      DO 15 I=1,100
      A(I)=I
   15 CONTINUE
```

This program segment will generate the integers from 1 to 100 and store then in the A array. Similarly a matrix may be generated without the necessity of providing data.

We have also discussed a method of reading arrays or input using the self-indexing technique.

```
READ(5,23)(A(I),I=1,50)
```

This will cause 50 numbers to be read as input with the READ statement executed only once.

Let us consider another form of input, using an Identifier for the lower limit or upper limit. In this example, we use an Identifier for the upper limit.

```
READ(5,18)L,(H(K),K=2,L)
```

A fixed point quantity L would be read establishing the upper limit. Then values 2 to L would be read.

If the value of L is 10, a total of 9 values would be read as input for the array.

When a READ statement is executed, the values being read are immediately assigned to their corresponding Identifiers in the list being read. Thus, a fixed point value read early in a list can be used as a subscript later in the list. For example:

```
READ(5,20)I,X(I)
```

When this statement is executed, two numbers will be read from a card. The first number, a fixed point quantity, will immediately become the subscript of the second number.

Many computers are also capable of processing a three-dimensional array. This must be specified in the program by a DIMENSION statement with three constants. The size of the array is determined by the product of the three constants.

CHAPTER NINE

LOGICAL CONTROL

As the reader has seen in the earlier chapters, FORTRAN statements are executed one after the other in physical order unless a change is directed by a logical control statement such as an IF or GO TO. The purpose of logical control is to alter the normal sequence of statement execution in a program. There are several types of branching statements,

a) Simple GO TO

b) Computed GO TO

c) Assigned GO TO

d) Arithmetic IF

e) Logical IF

SIMPLE GO TO

The form of the simple GO TO statement is

GO TO statement number

The simple GO TO statement provides an unconditional branch to one other statement in the program. Control is transferred to the statement which is denoted by a statement number.

```
10 READ(5,42)A,B,C,D
   .....
   .....
   .....
   GO TO 10
```

A number can be used as a statement number only once in a program. However, an arbitrary number of references or branches to any statement number may be made in the program.

Example:

```
20 READ(5,62)X,Y,Z
   .....
   .....
   .....
   GO TO 20
   .....
   .....
   .....
   GO TO 20
   .....
```

COMPUTED GO TO

A more sophisticated form of the GO TO that provides for conditional branching to any desired number of paths is the computed GO TO statement. The computed GO TO statement consists of the words GO TO followed by a pair of parentheses containing any desired listing of statement numbers separated by commas. The parentheses themselves are followed by a comma and a fixed point Identifier.

Example:

```
GO TO (60,15,20),L

GO TO (90,60,70,20,30,50,3),I
```

The value of the fixed point Identifier is determined elsewhere in the program. It must be greater than zero and not greater than the number of statement numbers enclosed in parentheses. In the examples above, L could not exceed 3 and I could not exceed 7.

The computer will proceed from the computed GO TO to the statement whose statement number appears in the list in the place corresponding to the value of the fixed point Identifier.

In the first example, if L equals 2, the computer would go to the second statement number, 15. In the second example, if I equals 3, the computer would proceed to the third statement number, 70.

Example: GO TO (60,15,20),L

If the computed value of L is 1, then control transfers to statement number 60. If the computed value of L is 2, then control transfers to statement number 15. If the computed value of L is 3, then control transfers to statement number 20.

Note that the value of the Identifier does not denote directly the statement number chosen for the next statement to be executed; rather, it denotes the position in the list.

```
.....
.....
READ(5,10)N
.....
.....
.....
.....
GO TO (5,4,3,2,1),N
```

If the value read for N is 5, the computer will be directed to go to statement number 1 rather than to statement number 5.

The list of statement numbers may be as long as desired and the same numbers may appear more than once in the list.

e.g. GO TO (15,20,25,15,30,35,15,40,.....),M

The program segment on the following page illustrates the use of the computed GO TO.

Example:

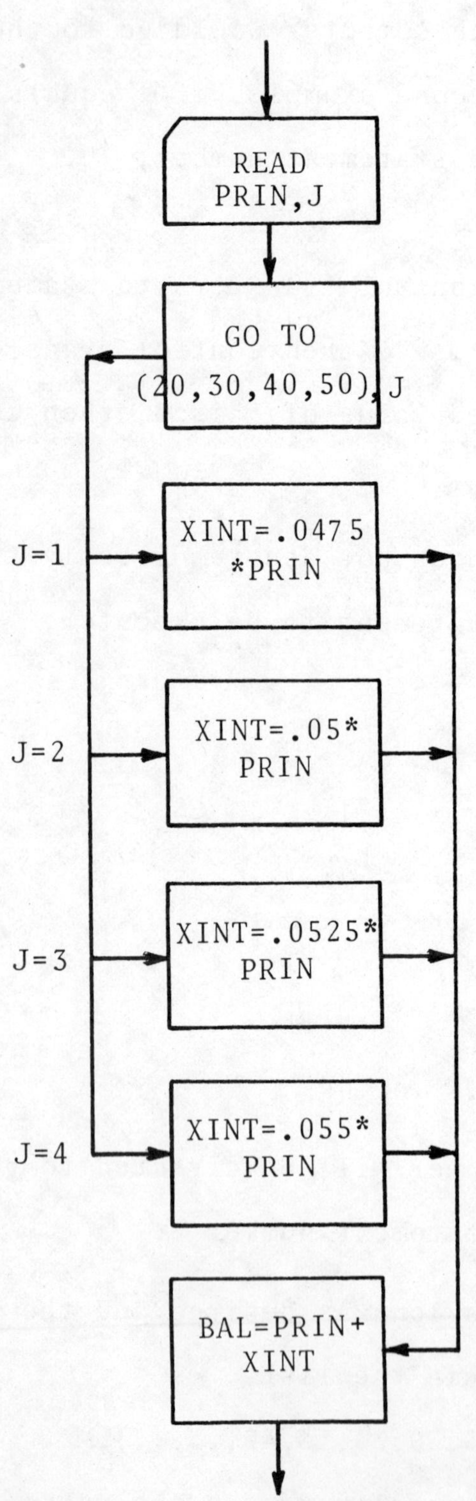


```
      .....
      .....
    5 READ(5,400) PRIN,J
  400 FORMAT(F10.4,I10)
      GO TO (20,30,40,50),J
   20 XINT=.0475*PRIN
      GO TO 101
   30 XINT=.05*PRIN
      GO TO 101
   40 XINT=.0525*PRIN
      GO TO 101
   50 XINT=.055*PRIN
  101 BAL=PRIN+XINT
      .....
```

ASSIGNED GO TO

A third form of the GO TO is the assigned GO TO. The assigned GO TO is similar to the computed GO TO in format and usage. It differs in that the fixed point Identifier follows immediately after the GO TO rather than after the parenthesized list of statement numbers. The Identifier is separated from the list of statement numbers by a comma.

```
GO TO N,(40,50,20)
GO TO JOB,(10,30,40,20,50)
```

The assigned GO TO is used in situations where the branch points can be pre-set in the program rather than be determined in the program as in the computed GO TO. When the assigned GO TO statement is executed, the computer will go next to one of the statements whose number is included in the parenthesized list. The choice is made according to the actual statement number which is currently "assigned" to the fixed point Identifier named in the GO TO statement. The assignment of the statement number to the fixed point Identifier is done by an ASSIGN statement. The form of the ASSIGN statement is the word ASSIGN followed by a statement number, the word TO, and the fixed point variable listed in the associated GO TO statement.

```
ASSIGN 40 TO N
ASSIGN 50 TO JOB
```

Normally more than one ASSIGN statement is used with an assigned GO TO, as illustrated in the program segment on the following page.

Example:

```
10 READ(5,28)X,Y
28 FORMAT(2F10.4)
   .....
   .....
   .....
   ASSIGN 20 TO N      ]  Branch to routine at 40
   GO TO 40            ]  with return set to 20
20 .....
   .....
   .....
   .....
   ASSIGN 30 TO N      ]  Branch to routine at 40
   GO TO 40            ]  with return set to 30
30 .....
   .....
   .....
   .....
   .....
   GO TO 10
40 .....               ]
   .....               ]
   .....               ]  Routine
   .....               ]
   GO TO N,(20,30)     ]
```

<u>ARITHMETIC IF</u>

The arithmetic IF statement causes transfer to one of three statements depending on the value (less than, equal to, or greater than zero) of an arithmetic expression. The form is:

IF(arithmetic expression)statement number,statement number,statement number

Examples:

```
IF(A+B) 22,13,19
IF(B**2-4.*A*C) 18,22,29
IF(27-I) 19,402,2
IF(X*Y) 15,20,15
```

The arithmetic expression is any legal FORTRAN arithmetic expression. The three statement numbers must appear somewhere in the program.

The arithmetic IF statement functions in the following manner:

The arithmetic expression is evaluted, resulting in a value less than, equal to, or greater than zero.

If the value is less than zero (negative), control is transferred to the statement labeled by the first statement number.

If the value is equal to zero, control is transferred to the statement labeled by the second statement number.

If the value is greater than zero (positive), control is transferred to the statement labeled by the third statement number.

The following program segment illustrates the use of the arithmetic IF.

```
 9 .....
   .....
   IF(B**2-4.*A*C) 18,22,29
22 .....
   .....
   GO TO 9
18 .....
   .....
   .....
   .....
   GO TO 9
29 .....
   .....
   .....
   GO TO 9
```

A flow chart for the arithmetic IF might appear as follows:

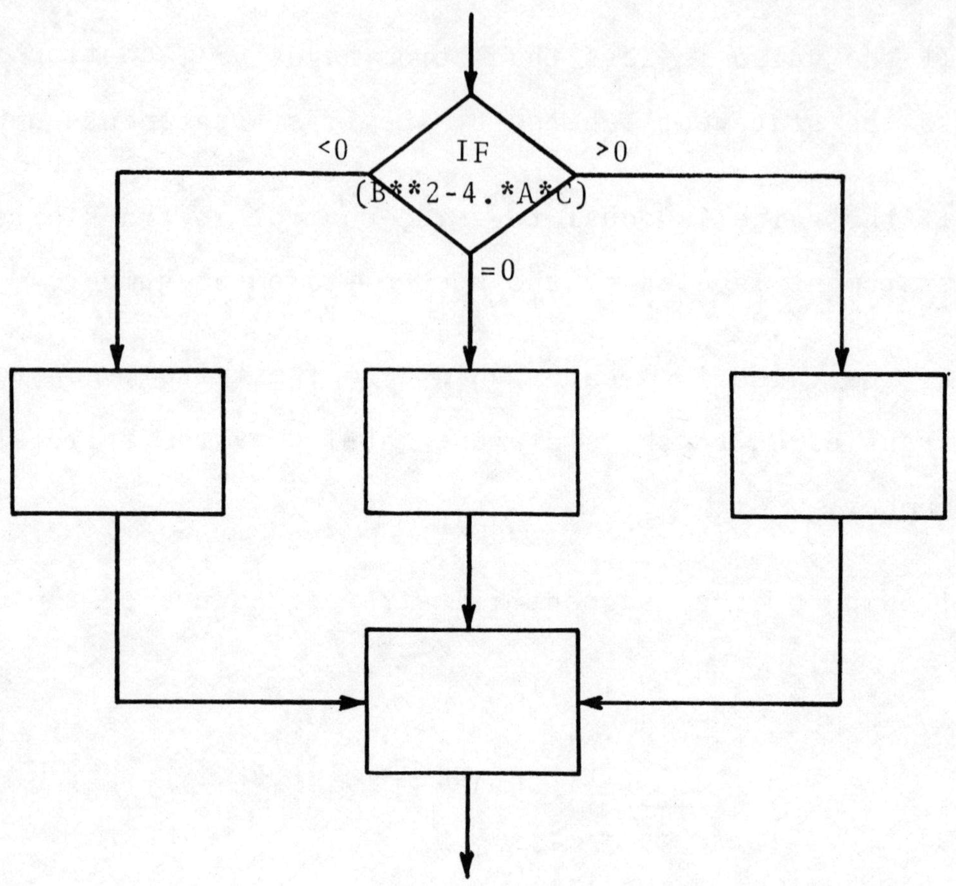

There are many variations to this diagram depending on the logical structure of the program.

LOGICAL IF

The logical IF statement causes a conditional transfer to one of two statements depending on the value (true or false) obtained from the evaluation of a logical expression. The form is:

```
IF(logical expression)statement
```

Examples:

```
IF(X.LT.Y) STOP
IF(A+B.EQ.7.0) GO TO 30
IF(I.LT.9) I=I+1
```

A logical expression in the form (e_1 relational operation symbol e_2) is always acceptable. The expressions e_1 and e_2 may be single variables or constants or more complicated arithmetic expressions, but both must be either real (floating point) or integer (fixed point).

The legal relational operation symbols are listed below:

Operation Symbol	Meaning	Mathematical Notation
.EQ.	Equal to	$=$
.NE.	Not equal to	$\neq$
.GT.	Greater than	$>$
.LT.	Less than	$<$
.GE.	Greater than or equal to	$\geq$
.LE.	Less than or equal to	$\leq$

The periods are part of the symbol.

The value of a logical expression is either true or false.

For example, if X=2.5 and Y=3.0.

The value of (X.LT.Y) is true
The value of (X.GT.Y) is false
The value of (X+Y.EQ.5.5) is true

The statement following the logical expression may be any executable statement except an IF or a DO statement.

The logical IF statement functions in the following manner:

The logical expression is evaluated, resulting in a value of either true or false.

If the logical expression is true, the statement immediately following the logical expression is executed. If this statement does not transfer control, the next statement is then executed.

If the logical expression is false, the statement following the logical expression is skipped and the next statement is executed.

For example:

```
IF(X.GT.Y) XP=X
K=K+1
```

If X is greater than Y, the value of X is assigned to XP and then K+1 is assigned to K.

If X is not greater than Y, the statement XP=X is skipped and K=K+1 is executed.

The use of the logical IF statement allows the programmer to combine the results of several comparisons in a single logical expression and to effect branching within the program.

If the programmer wishes to execute a statement following a logical expression when all of the series of conditions are met, he uses

.AND.

as illustrated below.

```
IF(A.EQ.C.AND.B.EQ.5.7)A=B+2.*C
```

The statement A=B+2.*C is executed only when both conditions are true. Otherwise, the next statement in sequence is executed.

If the programmer wishes to execute the statement following a logical expression when one or more of a series of conditions is met, he uses

.OR.

as illustrated below.

```
IF(A.EQ.C.OR.B.EQ.5.7)A=B+2.*C
```

The statement A=B+2.*C is executed when either condition is true. Otherwise the next statement in sequence is executed.

The .AND. and the .OR. may be used in the same logical expression. Parentheses may be used to indicate the order of operations desired.

Some of the variations in the use of the logical IF are illustrated by the following:

1)

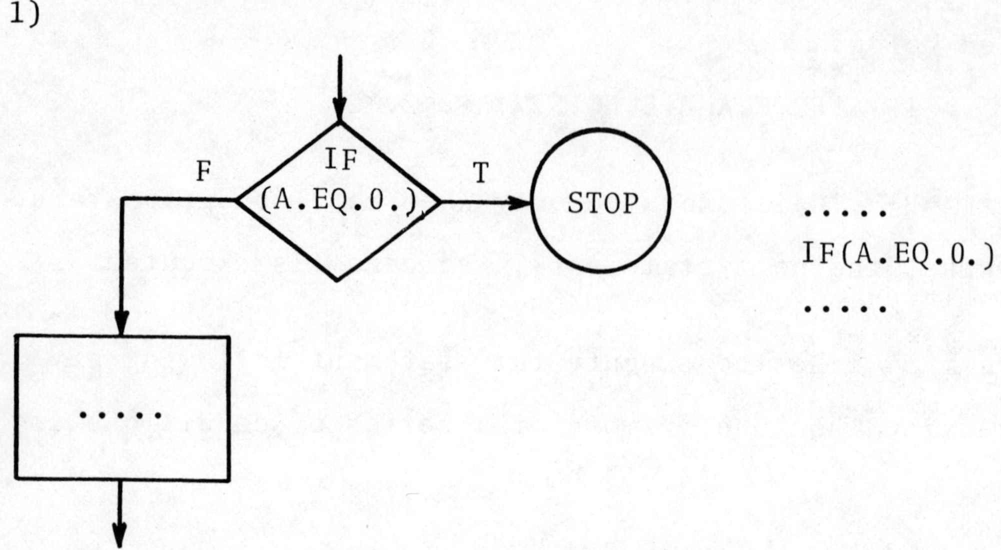


```
.....
IF(A.EQ.0.) STOP
.....
```

2)

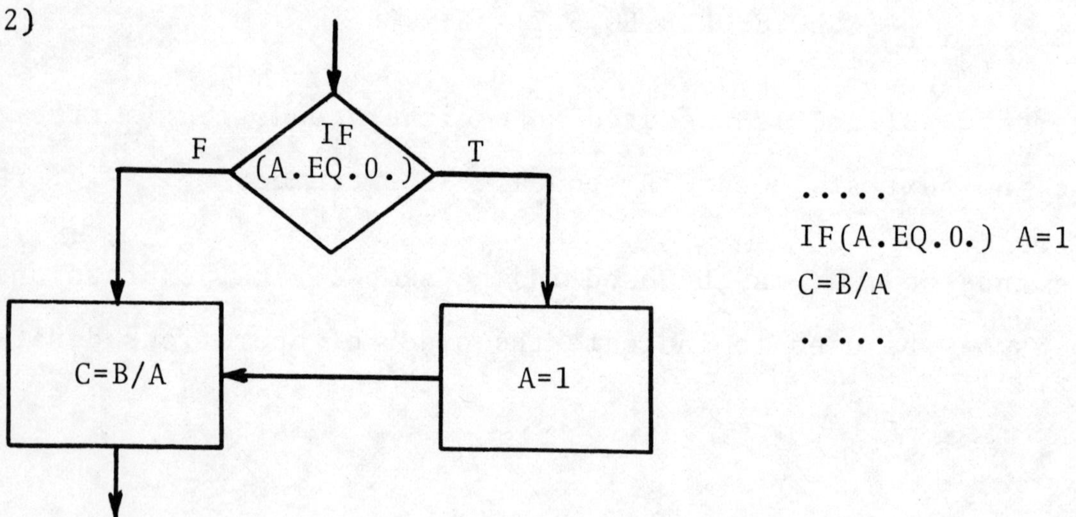


```
.....
IF(A.EQ.0.) A=1
C=B/A
.....
```

3)

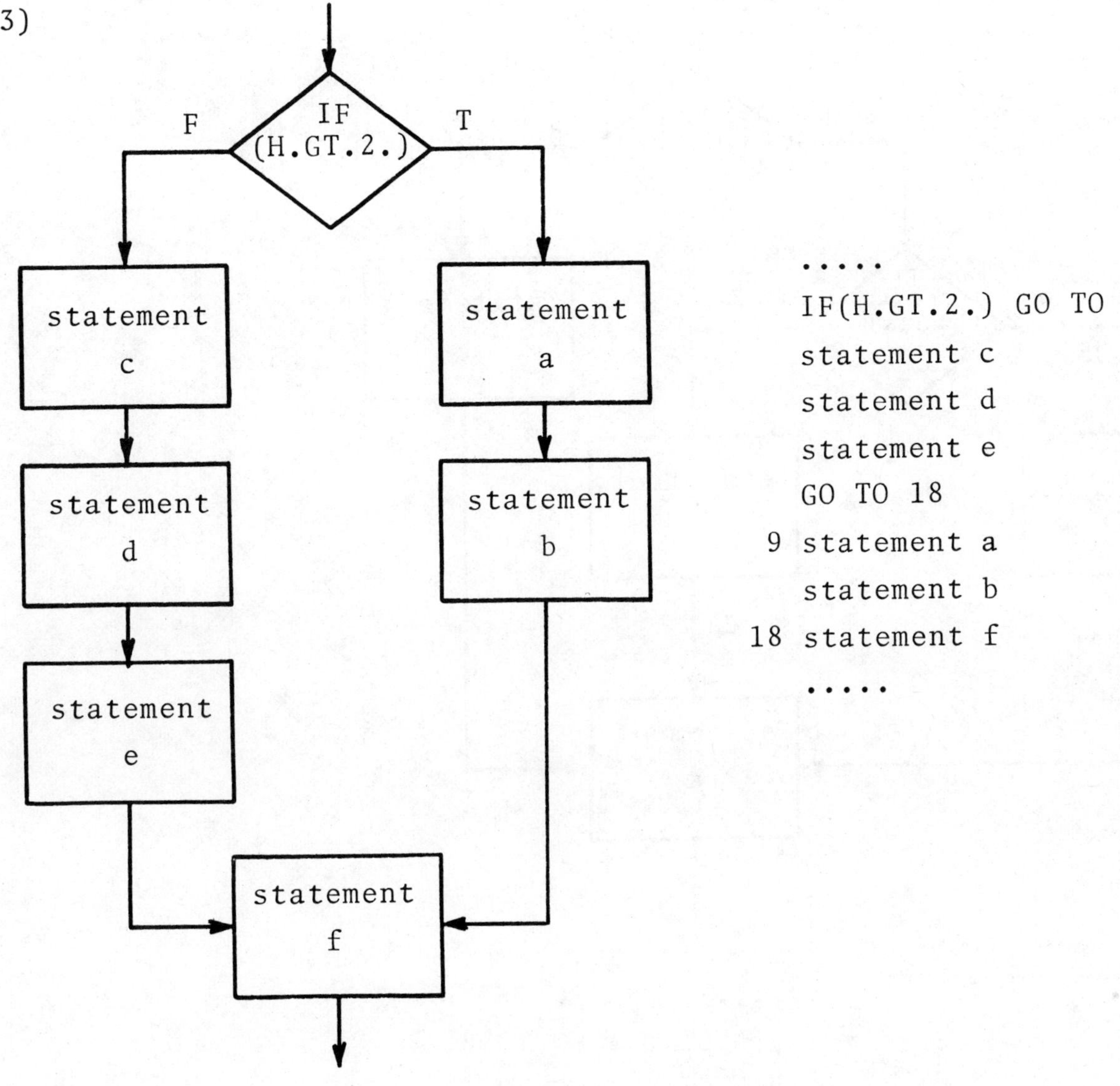


```
     .....
     IF(H.GT.2.) GO TO 9
     statement c
     statement d
     statement e
     GO TO 18
   9 statement a
     statement b
  18 statement f
     .....
```

4)

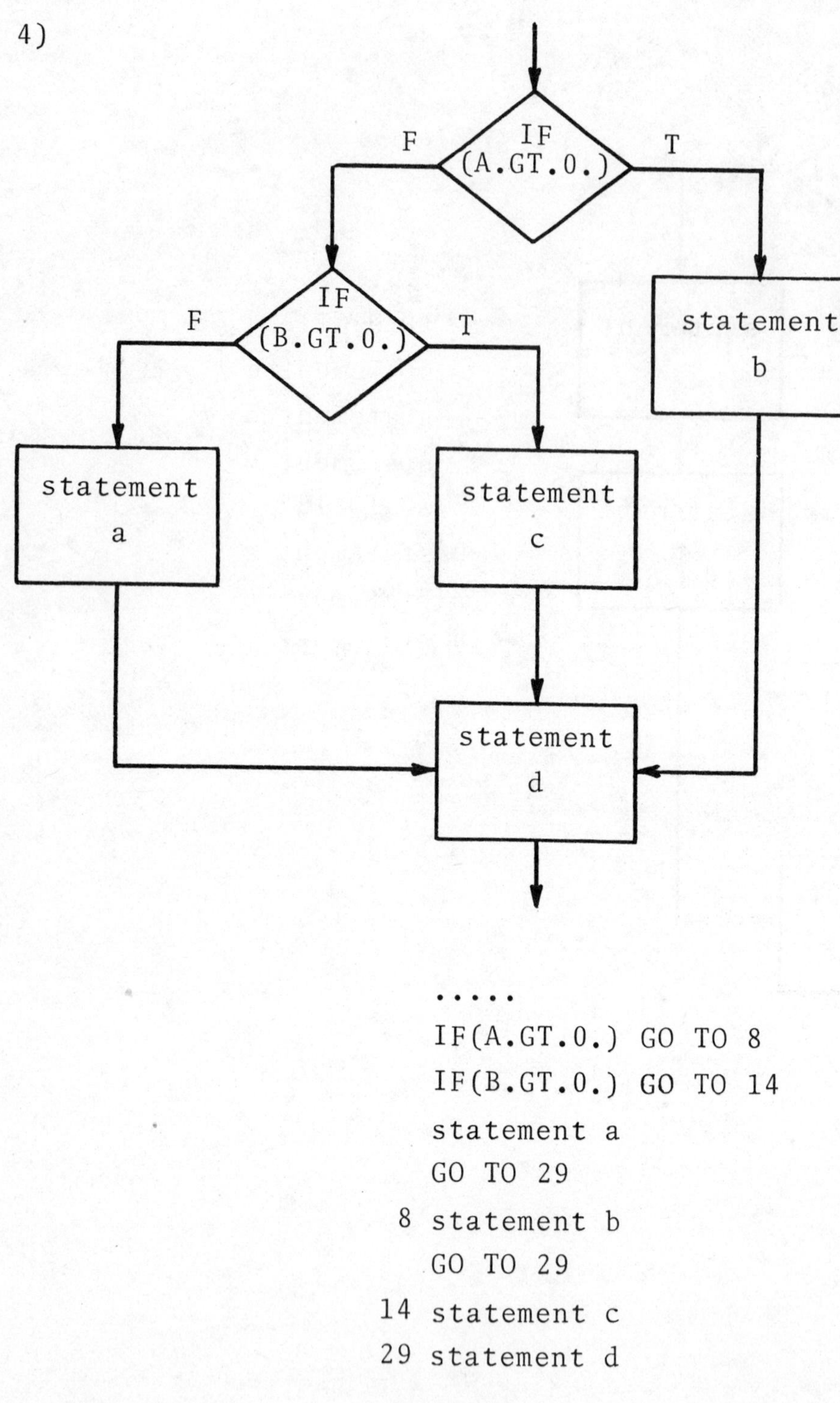


```
     .....
     IF(A.GT.0.) GO TO 8
     IF(B.GT.0.) GO TO 14
     statement a
     GO TO 29
   8 statement b
     GO TO 29
  14 statement c
  29 statement d
     .....
```

The above illustrate only a few of the many possible methods to use the logical IF to control the program logic.

CHAPTER TEN

ITERATIVE TECHNIQUES

One of the important features of the computer is its ability to accomplish iterative calculations - that is, to repeat a series of operations again and again. Iteration in FORTRAN is controlled by the DO statement, and for this reason, the DO statement is considered one of the most powerful statements in the language.

The DO statement and its operation have been discussed on an elementary level in Chapter Five. In order to discuss the DO statement in greater depth, the following definitions should be noted.

The DO statement in its most general form is

$$\text{DO n K}=m_1,m_2,m_3$$

n = a statement number defining the end of the loop;

K = an integer Identifier constituting the index;

m_1 = an integer Identifier or a positive integral constant defining the initial value, must be less than or equal to m_2;

m_2 = an integer Identifier or a positive integral constant defining the terminal value;

m_3 = an integer Identifier or a positive integral constant defining the increment

Note: m_1,m_2,m_3, are referred to as indexing parameters.

There are two ways of transferring control out of the range of a DO - a normal exit and a special exit.

A normal exit occurs when the statements within the range of the DO are repeatedly executed until the value of the index K exceeds the test value and control passes to the statement following the statement whose number is n. When a normal exit occurs, the DO has been satisfied.

A special exit occurs when a transfer-type statement (IF, GO TO, etc.) within the range of a DO transfers control to a statement outside the range of the DO.

Normal Exit from a DO loop:

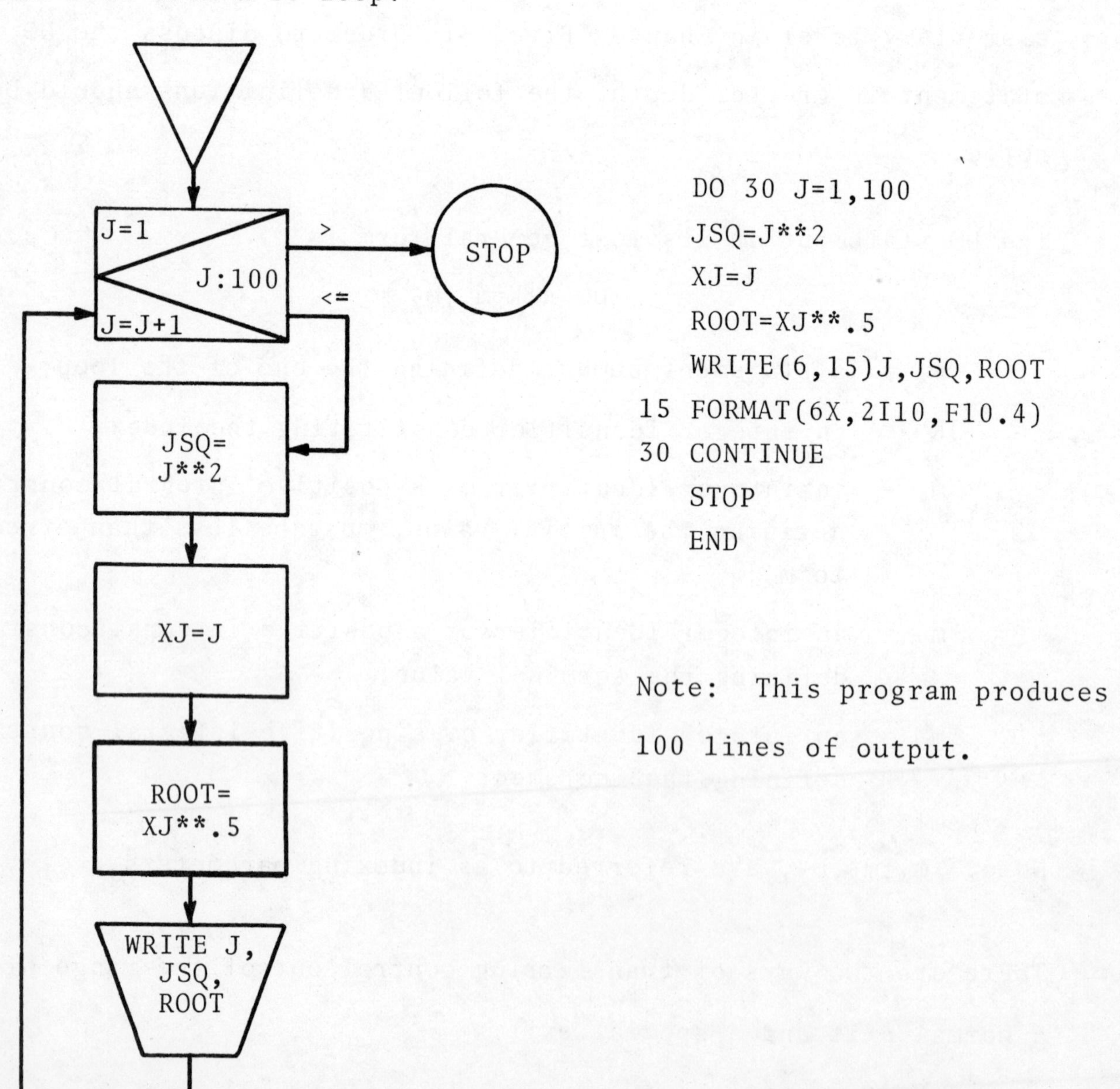


```
      DO 30 J=1,100
      JSQ=J**2
      XJ=J
      ROOT=XJ**.5
      WRITE(6,15)J,JSQ,ROOT
   15 FORMAT(6X,2I10,F10.4)
   30 CONTINUE
      STOP
      END
```

Note: This program produces 100 lines of output.

Special exit from a DO loop:

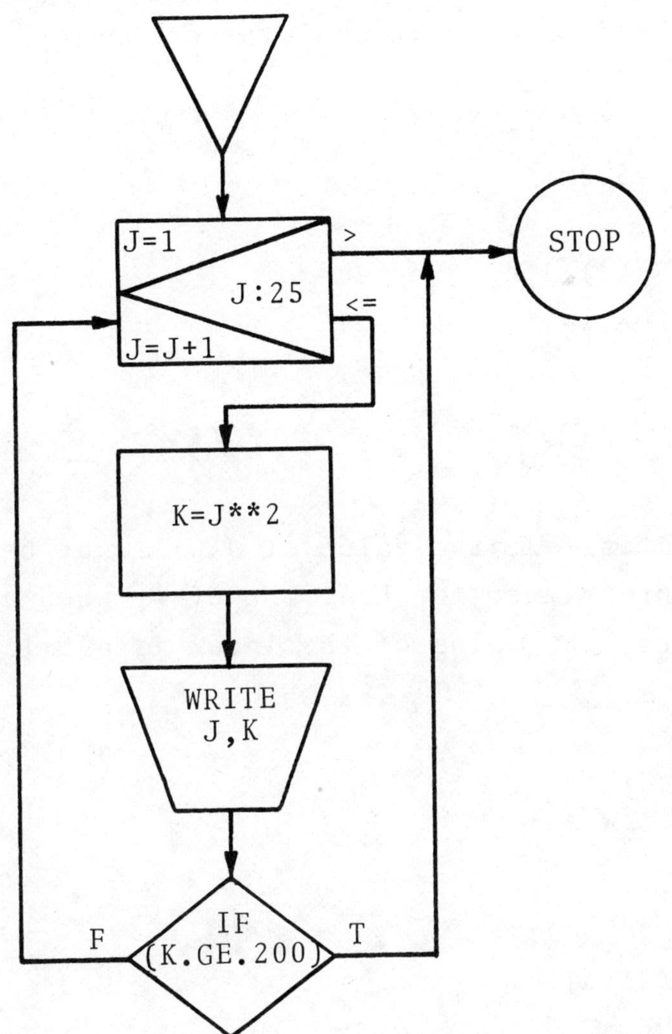


```
   DO 87 J=1,25
   K=J**2
   WRITE(6,42) J,K
42 FORMAT(6X,2I6)
   IF(K.GE.200) GO TO 8
87 CONTINUE
 8 STOP
   END
```

Note: This program produces 15 lines of output

When employing the DO in FORTRAN, the following rules must be observed:

1) When a normal exit occurs, the value of the index is undefined and may not be used in computations unless it is redefined.

```
      .....
      DO 20 J=5,20
      K=2**J
      WRITE(5,10) J,K
   10 FORMAT(6X,I8)
   20 CONTINUE
      L=J
      .....
```

Since the DO is satisfied, the value of J will not be available to the programmer for L=J. However, when a special exit occurs, the value of the index is available for computation.

```
      .....
      DO 50 J=1,20
      K=2**J
      IF(K.GT.100)GO TO 30
      WRITE(5,60) J,K
   60 FORMAT(2I10)
   50 CONTINUE
   30 L=J
      .....
```

Here the current value of J would be available for L=J because when K>100 a special exit occurs.

2) The index K or the indexing parameters (m_1,m_2,m_3) may not be redefined in the range of the DO. Thus the index or any of the parameters may not appear to the left of an equal sign or in an input list in any statement in the range of the DO.

3) The last statement in the range of a DO must not be a FORMAT, END, CALL, or DIMENSION statement.

4) The last statement in the range of a DO cannot be a transfer statement such as a GO TO or an IF.

5) The limits of an index may not exceed certain magnitudes. The programmer should determine the limitations for his installation.

6) One or more DO's may be included within the range of another DO statement. This is called nesting.

NESTED DO LOOPS

It is frequently necessary to write a program with a DO loop existing within another DO loop. The outer loop (defined by the first of the DO statements) is begun, and on its first pass gives control to the inner loop (defined by a DO statement within the range of the first). The inner loop processes itself completely until its upper limit is exceeded. Control is then returned to the outer loop and the outer loop starts on its second pass. On the second pass, the inner loop takes control again and processes itself completely a second time, etc. When the upper limit of the outer loop is exceeded, the computer proceeds to the next step of the program.

Just as there are rules governing the use of the single DO statement, there are also rules governing the use of nested DO's.

1) One cannot use the same index in both DO's of a nested DO; however, one may use the same index in two sequential loops.

2) Control may be transferred from a point inside of a DO loop to a point outside of the loop. However, if the transfer is back to the DO statement, the transfer initializes the index.

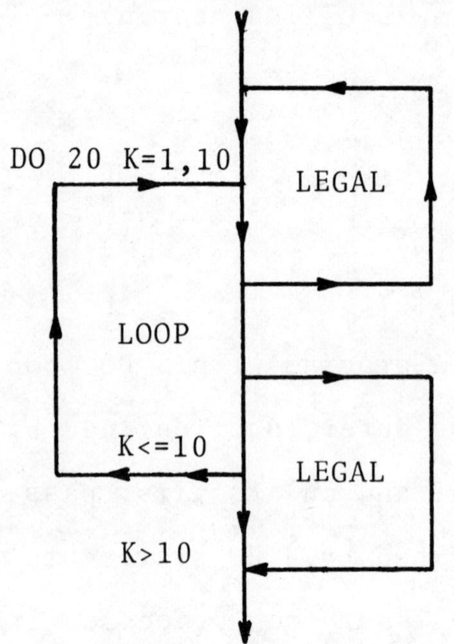

Control may be transferred to some previous statement in the program.

This is permissible, but it must be used with care. It results in starting the index back to K=1. This can result in an infinite loop.

Control may be transferred out of the loop. (special exit)

3) Transfer from a point outside of a DO loop to a point inside the DO loop is not allowed.

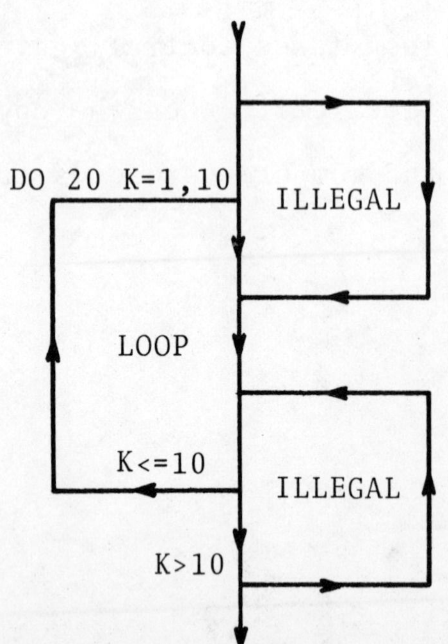

Transfers such as these would not allow the DO's to be correctly indexed.

4) In a nested DO loop all the statements of the inner DO must be within the range of the outer DO. Both may end in the same statement, but no overlapping is permitted.

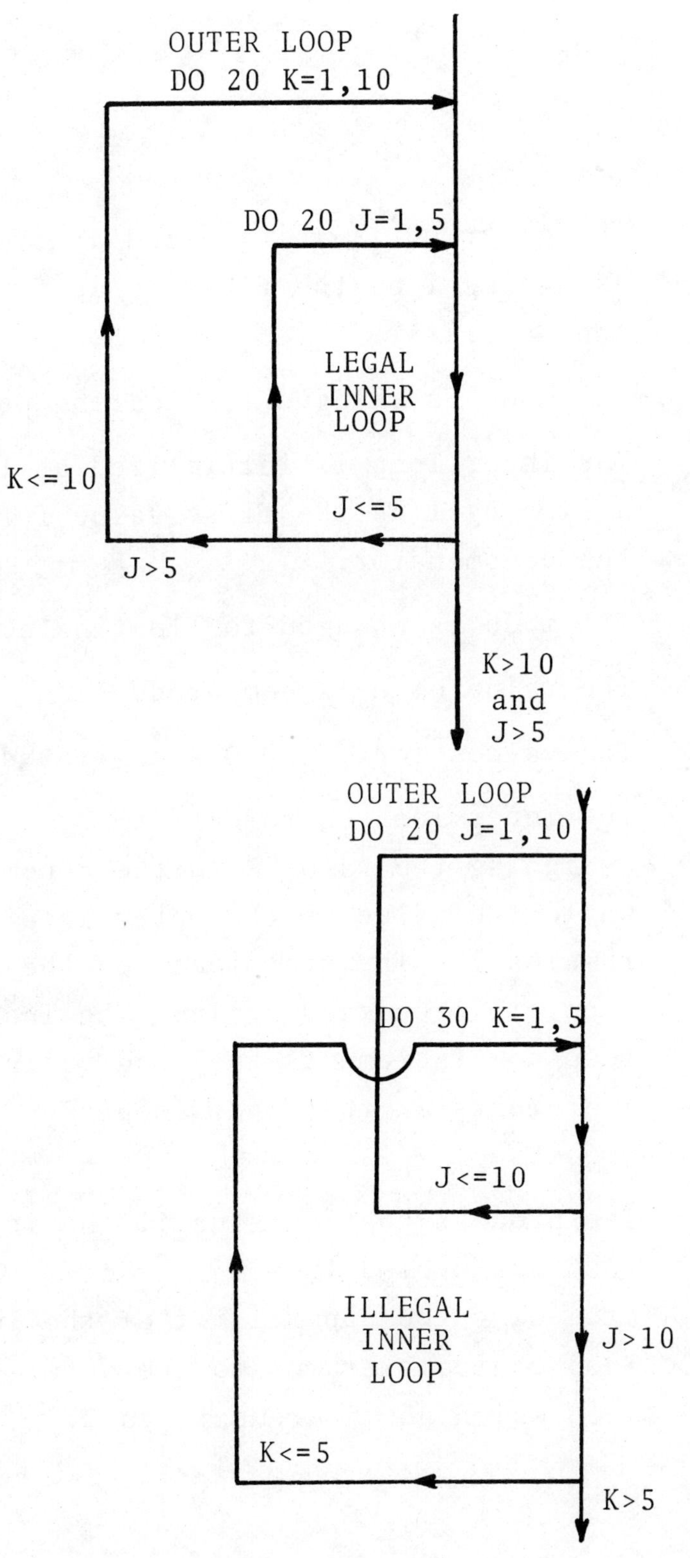

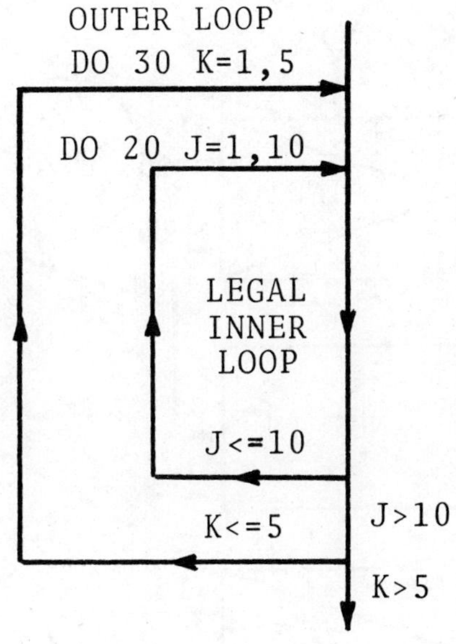

This in effect attempts to transfer control from outside of a loop to a point inside of the range of that loop.

The use of nested DO loops will be illustrated by a program directing the computer to generate a table showing the decimal equivalents of fractions where the numerators and denominators assume all the values between 1 and 16.

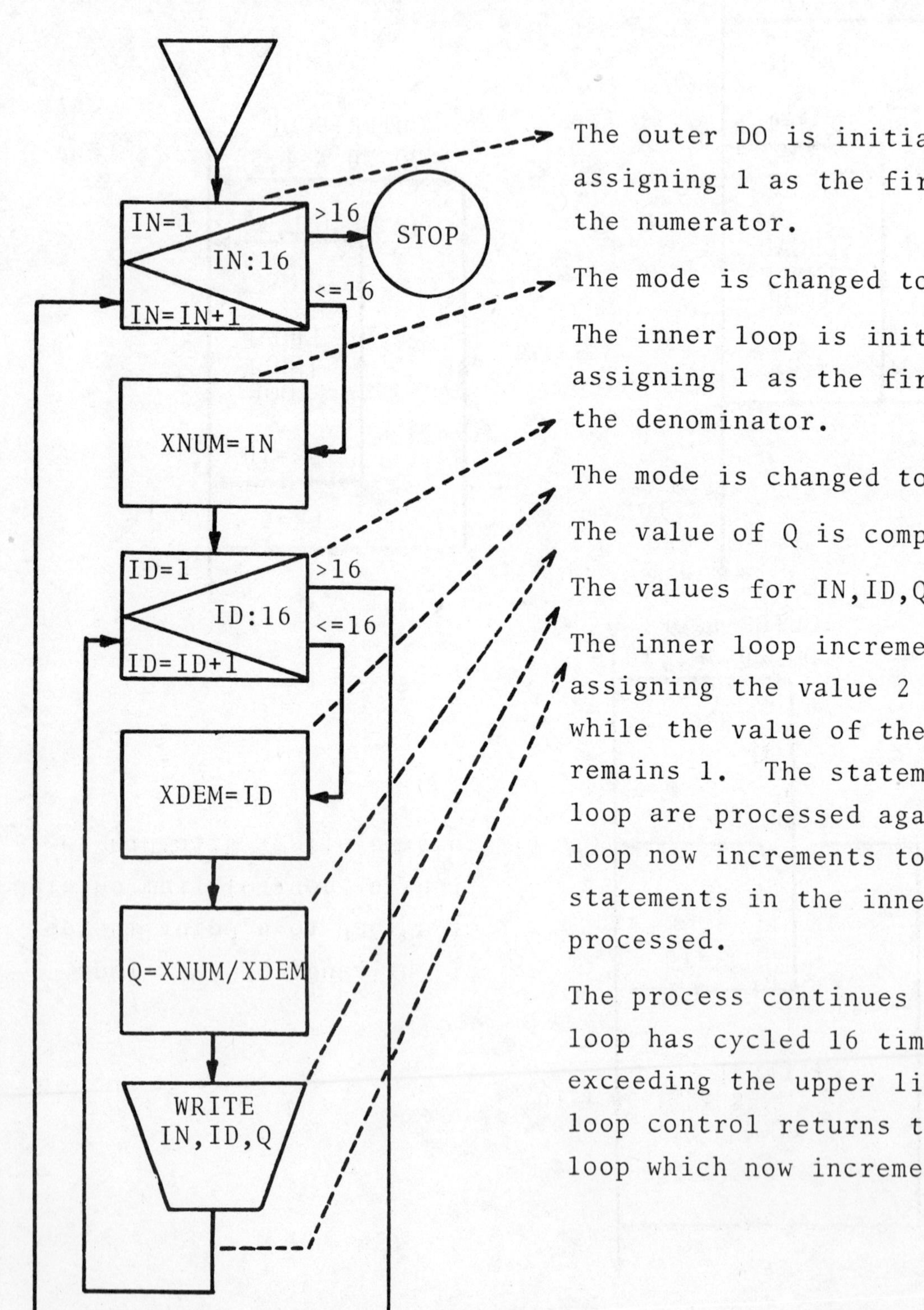

The outer DO is initialized at 1: assigning 1 as the first value for the numerator.

The mode is changed to floating point.

The inner loop is initialized at 1: assigning 1 as the first value for the denominator.

The mode is changed to floating point.

The value of Q is computed.

The values for IN,ID,Q are printed.

The inner loop increments to 2, assigning the value 2 to the denominator while the value of the outer loop remains 1. The statements of the inner loop are processed again. The inner loop now increments to 3 and again the statements in the inner loop are processed.

The process continues until the inner loop has cycled 16 times. Upon exceeding the upper limit of the inner loop control returns to the outer loop which now increments to 2.

The value of the inner loop is now initialized to 1 again and the inner loop is processed 16 times again with the numerator equal to 2.

The process continues until both loops have been satisfied.

Each time the outer loop increments once, the inner loop cycles 16 times and then passes control back to the outer loop.

When both loops have been exhausted, the program goes to STOP.

Note: This program produces 256 lines of output.

CODING:

```
   DO 99 IN=1,16
   XNUM=IN
   DO 99 ID=1,16
   XDEM=ID
   Q=XNUM/XDEM
   WRITE(6,82)IN,ID,Q
82 FORMAT(6X,2I10,F10.4)
99 CONTINUE
   STOP
   END
```

The use of three nested DO loops is illustrated in the following program.

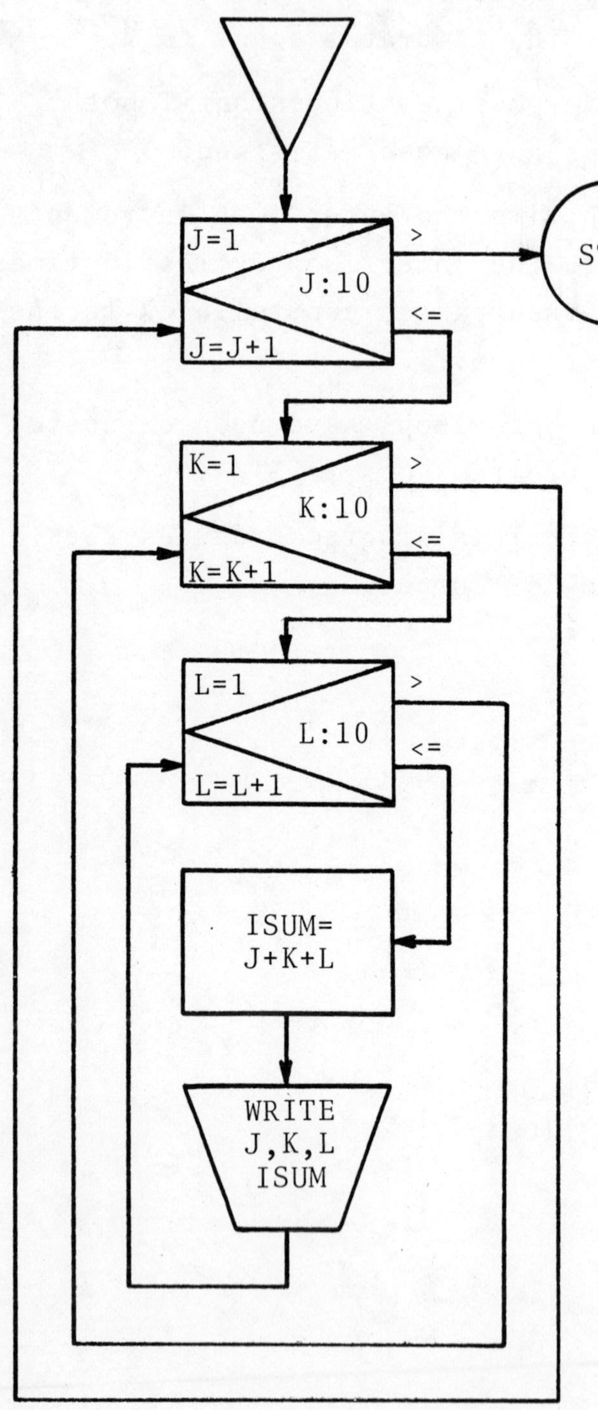

Coding:

```
      DO 20 J=1,10
      DO 20 K=1,10
      DO 20 L=1,10
      ISUM=J+K+L
      WRITE(6,10) J,K,L,ISUM
   10 FORMAT(1X,4I10)
   20 CONTINUE
      STOP
      END
```

Note the passing of control by examining the output.

Line #	Output			
1	1	1	1	3
2	1	1	2	4
3	1	1	3	5
4	1	1	4	6
.	.	.	.	.
10	1	1	10	12
.	.	.	.	.
15	1	2	5	8
.	.	.	.	.
100	1	10	10	21
101	2	1	1	4
.	.	.	.	.
1000	10	10	10	30

Note: This program will produce 1000 lines of output.

CHAPTER ELEVEN

SUBPROGRAMS

The previous chapters have discussed the three basic elements of scientific programming languages - arithmetic, control, and input/output - as they are programmed in the FORTRAN language. The features presented in this chapter give considerable added flexibility in the FORTRAN language through subprograms, which are defined as program segments that are executed under control of some other program. These subprograms are usually tailored to perform some oft-repeated set of operations. A subprogram is written only once, but may be used again and again in a single program or may be used in many different programs. In either case, duplication of effort is avoided by eliminating the need for re-writing program segments to perform these common operations.

LIBRARY FUNCTIONS

One set of subprograms provided for FORTRAN users is called a library and the programs contained in the library are called library functions. The use of these library programs is very simple and easily explained.

Through a series of basic arithmetic statements, it is possible for a program to perform more complicated mathematical functions.

Thus we could direct the computer to find an approximate value of the trigonometric sine of angle X using the Assignment statement:

```
SINX=A-A**3/(3.*2.*1.)+A**5/(5.*4.*3.*2.*1.)-A**7/(7.*6.*5.*4.*3.*2.*1.)
```

Fortunately, in order to save the programmer time and work, the computer has already been programmed so that the programmer can merely write:

```
Y=SIN(X)
```

and the computer will produce the sine of angle X and assign the value to Y. This built-in-function allowing the programmer to get the sine of the angle X merely by writing Y=SIN(X) is called a subprogram or Library function. FORTRAN versions have at least seven of these subprograms (Sine, Cosine, Exponential, Logarithm, Square Root, Arc-tangent, and Absolute Value).

Every Library function has a particular name associated with it. If the programmer wishes to use the subprogram, all he needs to do is use its name in a FORTRAN expression in the same manner as he would with an Identifier. However, care must be taken to use the exact FORTRAN name. Furthermore, the name of a Library function may not be used in any expression to represent anything other than its function.

Library functions are programs which compute some functional relation of a single quantity, called an argument.

In Y=SIN(X), the argument is the angle X, whose sine is to be computed. Note that the argument is enclosed in parentheses. The value of X would have to be given in radians, not degrees.

The value of the argument is the quantity that the computer uses to compute the desired result. The argument itself may be a constant, an Identifier, any legal expression, or even another function.

e.g.

```
Y=SIN(3.14159)
Y=SIN(A**2+B**2)
Y=SIN(SQRT(X))
```

With nested functions, the innermost function is evaluated first for the use of the outer function.

e.g.

```
Y=SIN(SQRT(ALOG(X**2)))
```

The computer would first square X, then find the log of the square of X, take the square root of the log, and finally find the sine of the square root value.

The table on the following page lists the common Library functions available to systems using FORTRAN: the mathematical notation, the exact FORTRAN names, and the restrictions on the values for the arguments.

However, computer installations have variations in their libraries and the programmer should inquire at the computer center to find out what library programs are available and exactly what restrictions exist concerning the programs.

FUNCTION	MATHEMATICAL NOTATION	FORTRAN NAME	ARGUMENTS
Trigonometric Sine	sin A	SIN(A)	Real (in radians)
Trigonometric Cosine	cos A	COS(A)	Real (in radians)
Arctangent	$\tan^{-1} A$	ATAN(A)	Real
Square Root	$\sqrt{A}$	SQRT(A)	Real >=0
Exponential	e^A	EXP(A)	Real
Natural Logarithm	logA	ALOG(A)	Real >0
Common Logarithm	$\log_{10} A$	ALOG10(A)	Real >0
Absolute Value	$\|A\|$ $\|K\|$	ABS(A) IABS(K)	Real Integer

The following program will demonstrate the use of Library functions. It will find the square roots of a set of numbers read into the computer from cards.

```
 5 READ(5,10) A
10 FORMAT(F10.4)
   B=ABS(A)
   ROOT=SQRT(B)
   IF(A)15,25,35
35 WRITE(6,20) A,ROOT
20 FORMAT(6X,19HTHE SQUARE ROOT OF ,F10.4,8H IS +/- ,F10.4/)
   GO TO 5
15 WRITE(6,30) A,ROOT
30 FORMAT(6X,19HTHE SQUARE ROOT OF ,F10.4,8H IS +/- ,F10.4,2H I/)
   GO TO 5
25 STOP
   END
```

OUTPUT:

```
THE SQUARE ROOT OF     2.0000 IS +/-     1.4142
THE SQUARE ROOT OF    -3.0000 IS +/-     1.7321 I
THE SQUARE ROOT OF   158.0716 IS +/-    12.5727
THE SQUARE ROOT OF  -145.2937 IS +/-    12.0538 I
```

Let us review some facts we should now be aware of:

1. A function is recognized by its name.
2. A function name appearing in a FORTRAN expression results in the execution of the subprograms which have been previously written.
3. A function name has 1 to 6 characters - the first of which is alphabetic and determines the mode of the function.

Library functions represent only one type of subprogram which may be used in FORTRAN programs. Additional types of subprograms, each having a special use in FORTRAN are:

Arithmetic statement function

FUNCTION subprogram

and SUBROUTINE subprogram

ARITHMETIC STATEMENT FUNCTION

The Arithmetic statement function is used where no Library function or built-in function is available. A distinctive characteristic is that the Assignment statement subprogram is not written as a separate program as the other subprograms are but is written as one statement immediately preceding the first executable statement of the program. It applies only to the program in which it appears.

The general form is:

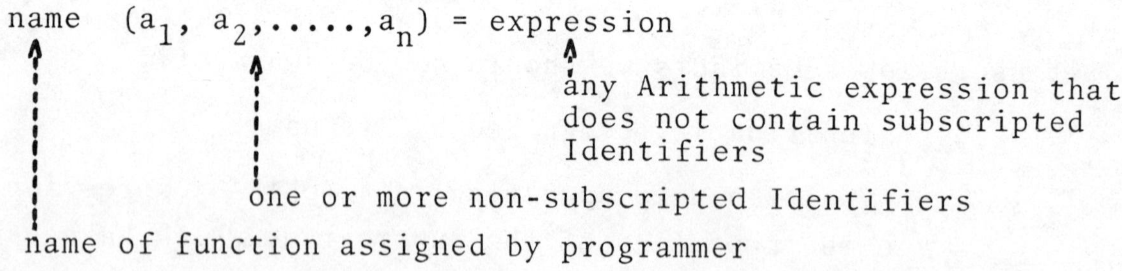

Since the Arithmetic statement function is written by a programmer for his special application, it follows that each Arithmetic statement may be different.

Simply stated an Arithmetic statement function is a subprogram written by the programmer in FORTRAN. A particular computation, one statement long, may be required at several different points in the program. For instance, suppose at several points in a program it is necessary to compute a root of a quadratic equation. Instead of writing instructions at each of the points, we can write an Arithmetic statement function once as follows:

```
QUADIF(A,B,C)=(-B+(B**2-4.0*A*C)**.5)/(2.0*A)
```

Thus at each point where a root is to be computed the programmer would use only the function name for the root, and the root would be computed and substituted.

We could define QUADIF(A,B,C) as above and later we could write:

```
X=QUADIF(A,B,C)
```

The root would be evaluated, based on current values of A, B, and C and the root would be assigned to X. The function statement is written only once but may be called any number of times we desire.

The Arithmetic statement function is an Arithmetic statement. Therefore the rules pertaining the Identifiers still apply. Specifically the name is limited to six characters - the first one alphabetic - and the first character determines the mode.

If a function cannot be expressed in one statement as required for the Arithmetic statement function, the programmer may write a subprogram containing as many statements as necessary to fully define the functional relationship desired. In this case the programmer would use either a FUNCTION subprogram or a SUBROUTINE subprogram.

FUNCTION SUBPROGRAM

The FUNCTION subprogram is itself a complete program; that is, it is written separately from any program which uses it and even has its own END statement. It is a completely separate segment of programming from the program which makes use of the function. It is used like a Library function; that is, it is a previously written program which is executed wherever its name appears in another program.

The general form of the FUNCTION subprogram is:

```
FUNCTION name (a1,a2,.....an)
.....
.....
name=.....
.....
.....
.....
.....
.....
RETURN
END
```

The FUNCTION subprogram is distinguished from an ordinary program by the very first statement in the program. A special statement is used, beginning with the word FUNCTION followed by its name, an open parenthesis, a list of arguments and a closed parenthesis. The FUNCTION statement is followed by any combination of statements needed to properly define the functional relationship and the single result which becomes the value of the function. When the FUNCTION subprogram has finished its task of computing its value, the RETURN statement (consisting of the word RETURN) signals the computer to go back to the other program. Finally, the END statement is required.

An example of a FUNCTION subprogram which produces the square root of a positive real argument follows:

```
      FUNCTION SQR(A)
      R=A/2.0
      DO 30 J=1,500
      SQR=.5*(R+A/R)
      IF(ABS(SQR**2-A)/A-0.000001)20,30,30
   30 R=SQR
   20 RETURN
      END
```

A FUNCTION subprogram is called by writing in an expression the function name followed by parentheses enclosing an argument or arguments separated by commas.

Thus: `X=(-B+SQR(D))/(2.*A)`

Functions of this third type have the same naming rules as the other two function types - that is, it has the same naming rules as ordinary Identifiers. The mode of the FUNCTION subprogram is also determined in the same way as the mode of the Arithmetic statement functions.

The arguments specified in the FUNCTION statement are dummy variables. This means that their names are used in the subprogram without definition of value, and the value used for any particular execution will be supplied by the statement in the other program. For instance, in the example the variable A was the dummy variable and anywhere the name A appeared in the FUNCTION the value of the argument in the other program would be used even if its name were not A. For this reason it is important to make certain that the arguments listed in the other program agree in number and mode with the arguments listed in the FUNCTION.

SUBROUTINE SUBPROGRAM

The fourth type of subprogram, the SUBROUTINE, is similar to the FUNCTION in many ways: the naming rules are the same, they both require a RETURN statement and an END statement, and they both contain the same sort of dummy argument variables.

Like the FUNCTION, the SUBROUTINE is also a set of commonly used operations grouped in subprogram form to be used again and again without re-writing, but it does not restrict itself to a single value for the result, as does the FUNCTION. In fact, a SUBROUTINE can be used for almost any operation with as many results as desired. Since the SUBROUTINE does not have just a single result, the manner in which the SUBROUTINE is called into action is different from the way the FUNCTION is called into action.

The SUBROUTINE is called by a special statement: the CALL statement, which consists of the word CALL followed by the name of the subprogram and its parenthesized list of arguments. For example:

```
CALL TAREA(X,Y,Z,A,I)
```

The general form of a SUBROUTINE subprogram is:

SUBROUTINE name ($a_1, a_2, \ldots\ldots a_n$)

.....

.....

RETURN

END

The arguments take on values passed from the calling program to the subprogram.

Let us consider this example of a SUBROUTINE subprogram which examines the values of A, B, and C to determine if they form the sides of a triangle. If they do TB is defined as the area of the triangle, and K is defined as 1. But if they do not, TB and K are defined as 0.0 and 2 respectively.

SUBPROGRAM

```
SUBROUTINE TAREA(A,B,C,TB,K)
TB=0.0
K=2
IF (A.GE.B+C) RETURN
IF (B.GE.A+C) RETURN
IF (C.GE.A+B) RETURN
S=.5*(A+B+C)
TB=SQRT(S*(S-A)*(S-B)*(S-C))
K=1
RETURN
END
```

Values may be communicated between a calling program and a SUBROUTINE subprogram by the arguments listed in the CALL statement and those listed in the SUBROUTINE statement. The two argument lists must agree in the following:

1. Order of arguments is the same from left to right.
2. Type of arguments must correspond.
3. Equal number of arguments in both lists.

In our program we have seen that when a RETURN statement is executed the arguments in the CALL statement take on the same value definition as the current values of the corresponding arguments listed in the SUBROUTINE statement.

Let us consider a program segment with communication between a calling program and the subprogram.

CALLING PROGRAM

```
      .....
      I=2
      A(I)=2.0
      X=0.3
      Y=0.7
      CALL ZEBRA(1,Z,A(I),X+Y,W)
      S=Z+A(I)
      .....
      END
```

SUBPROGRAM

```
      SUBROUTINE ZEBRA(N,P,Q,R,S)
      GO TO (8,10),N
    8 P=5.0*R-1.0
      Q=Q+1.0
    9 RETURN
   10 .....
      RETURN
      END
```

Let us examine the values passed between the two programs.

EXECUTION OF CALL ZEBRA

CALLING PROGRAM	SUBROUTINE
1	N is 1
Z is undefined	P is undefined
A(I) is 2.0	Q is 2.0
X+Y is 1.0	R is 1.0
W is undefined	S is undefined

EXECUTION OF 9 RETURN

SUBROUTINE	CALLING PROGRAM
N is 1	1
P is 4.0	Z is 4.0
Q is 3.0	A(I) is 3.0
R is 1.0	X+Y is undefined
S is undefined	W is undefined

The value of S would then be computed as 3.0+4.0 or 7.0.

SECTION THREE

APPENDIX I

PRACTICE PROBLEMS

All of the problems contained in this series can be solved through FORTRAN programming. Only the most elementary knowledge of the FORTRAN language is required.

A few of these problems require a knowledge of first-year high school algebra, but most problems require no mathematical training.

An attempt has been made to arrange the series in order of difficulty; however, since the difficulty of any problem depends on the background and aptitude of the person attempting to solve it, our arrangement should be considered with reservations. Therefore, you should not assume that difficulty with a particular problem will imply greater difficulty with succeeding problems.

1. Area of a square

   Find the area of any square by the formula, $A = s^2$.

2. Area of a rectangle

   Find the area of any rectangle by the formula, $A = lw$.

3. Volume of a cylinder

   Find the volume of any cylinder when the radius of the base and the height of the cylinder are known.

   The formula is $V=\Pi r^2 h$

   Use 3.14 as the value for Π.

4. Squares of integers 1 to 25

Write a program which will generate a two column table showing, in the first column, the integers 1 to 25, and in the second column, the square of each integer.

5. Daily pay

A man takes a job for thirty days. His pay for the first day is \$0.01; his pay for the second day is double, or \$0.02; for the third day, \$0.04; for the fourth day, \$0.08. Each day's pay is determined by the previous day's pay multiplied by two. The program should generate a table which will show his pay for each of the thirty days.

6. Fahrenheit to Centigrade table

The formula for converting Fahrenheit values to Centigrade is:

$$C = \frac{5}{9}(F-32)$$

Write a program that will generate a two column table showing, in the first column, all the <u>even</u> Fahrenheit values from 2 to 50 inclusive, and in the second column, each corresponding Centigrade value.

7. Finding the mean of ten numbers

Determine the sum of ten numbers, and divide by 10 to obtain the mean, or average, of the numbers.

8. Compound interest

The formula for compound interest is $A = P(1+\frac{I}{C})^{NC}$ where

A represents the amount (principal + interest)
N represents the number of years
C represents the number of conversions per year
I represents the yearly rate of interest
P represents the principal

The program should determine the value of A, when the other values are known.

9. Sum and last term of an Arithmetic Progression

Find the sum and last term of any Arithmetic Progression.

Let A represent the first term
Let D represent the common difference
Let N represent the number of terms
Let L represent the last term
Let S represent the sum of the terms

Then the formula for the last term is $L = A + D\ (N-1)$

The formula for the sum of the terms is $S = \frac{N\ (A + L)}{2}$

Example: The progression is 1, 3, 5, 7, 9.

Therefore,

$A = 1$
$D = 2$
$N = 5$

$L = A + D\ (N - 1)$ $\qquad S = \frac{N\ (A + L)}{2}$

$L = 1 + 2\ (5 - 1)$ $\qquad S = \frac{5\ (1 + 9)}{2}$

$L = 1 + 8$ $\qquad S = \frac{50}{2}$

$L = 9$ $\qquad S = 25$

10. Sum and last term of a Geometric Progression

Find the sum and last term of any Geometric Progression.

Let L represent the last term
Let A represent the first term
Let N represent the number of terms
Let R represent the common ratio
Let S represent the sum of the terms

Then the formula for the last term is $L = AR^{(N - 1)}$

The formula for the sum of the terms is $S = \frac{A - RL}{1 - R}$

Example: The progression is 2, 6, 18, 54.

Therefore,

$$A = 2$$
$$R = 3$$
$$N = 4$$

$$L = AR^{(N-1)} \qquad S = \frac{A - RL}{1 - R}$$

$$L = (2)3^{(4-1)} \qquad S = \frac{2 - 3(54)}{1 - 3}$$

$$L = (2)3^3 \qquad S = \frac{2 - 162}{-2}$$

$$L = (2)(27) \qquad S = \frac{-160}{-2}$$

$$L = 54 \qquad S = 80$$

11. Solution of $AX^2 + BX + C = 0$

Solve any second degree equation in one variable. The quadratic formula is:

$$X = \frac{-B \pm \sqrt{B^2 - 4AC}}{2A}$$

12. Solution of $AX + BY = C$ and $DX + EY = F$

Write a program that will solve any pair of simultaneous equations in two variables:

$$AX + BY = C$$
$$DX + EY = F$$

13. Finding the divisors of an integer

Write a program which will list all the integers which are divisors of a chosen integer.

14. Finding the primes 1 to 100

Write a program that will generate a list of all the prime numbers from 1 to 100.

15. Illegal cancellation

The equality $\frac{16}{64} = \frac{1}{4}$ is a result which can be obtained by the cancellation of the 6 in the numerator and denominator. Find all the cases in which AB/BC = A/C, for A, B, and C integers between 1 and 9 inclusive. Do not consider obvious special cases, such as 22/22, 33/33, etc.

16. Four digit numbers

The four digit number 3025 has the following property: If the number formed by considering only the first two digits (30) is added to the number formed by considering only the last two digits (25), the total will be 55; and if this number (55) is squared, the result will be the original number.

$$(55)^2 = 3025$$

Find all four digit numbers having this property. Do not check numbers beyond 9900, since 9901 would be arranged as,

$$99 + 01 = 100 \text{ and } (100)^2 = 10000$$

which is a five digit number.

17. Loan repayment

A loan of $1000 is to be repaid at the rate of $100 per month. The interest is charged at the rate of 1% on the unpaid balance each month. The program should generate a four column table showing the payment number, the balance, the interest for each month, and the amount paid on the principal each month. The new balance for each month is obtained by subtracting the amount paid on the principal from the old balance.

18. Mortgage problem

A $17,000 mortgage is to be repaid at the rate of $200 per month. The interest is charged at the rate of 6% each year, calculated each month. The program should be designed to generate a four column table which will show the payment number, the balance, the interest for each month, and the amount paid on the principal for each month. The new balance for each month is obtained by subtracting the amount paid on the principal from the old balance.

19. Addition table

Have the computer print out a table of addition facts. Let each of the two numbers to be added vary from one to ten. The output can be made to appear as follows by using a FORMAT statement:

```
 1 +  1 =  2
 1 +  2 =  3
   .....
 1 + 10 = 11
 2 +  1 =  3
 2 +  2 =  4
   .....
 2 + 10 = 12
   .....
10 + 10 = 20   (last line of output)
```

20. Payroll problem

Write a program to do a payroll, where the input consists of the hourly rate, the numbers of hours worked, the pension rate, the income tax rate, the amount of bond deduction, and the name of the employee.

The output should include gross pay, pension deduction, bond deduction, income tax deduction, take home or net pay, and employee name.

Note: The name of the employee may be deleted from the program.

21. Grade point average

In a certain school offering both "HONORS" courses and "REGULAR" courses, the letter grades A, B, C, D, and F are used to indicate achievement. To determine a student's grade point average, the following weights are used:

LETTER GRADE	POINT VALUE "HONORS"	POINT VALUE "REGULAR"
A	5	4
B	4	3
C	3	2
D	1	1
F	0	0

Write a program that will accept as input the <u>number</u> of "REGULAR" and "HONORS" letter grades received, and exhibit as output the student's grade point average. The program may be written with or without the name of the student.

22. Perfect numbers

In mathematics, a number is considered to be perfect if the sum of all of its divisors (except itself) is equal to the original number.

Example: The divisors of 6 are 1, 2, and 3.

$$1 + 2 + 3 = 6$$

Write a program that will determine all perfect numbers from 1 to 100, and which will exhibit as output all the divisors of the number (except itself), and the perfect number.

23. Sorting problem

Write a program which will arrange in ascending order any number of three digit numbers (up to 999). You may assume that no two of the numbers are equal.

24. Farmer problem

A farmer with $100 goes to market to buy 100 head of stock. Prices are as follows: calves, $10 each; pigs, $3 each; chickens, $0.50 each. He gets 100 head for his $100. How many of each does he buy? Assume that he buys at least one of each.

25. Monkey problem

There are three pirates and a monkey on a desert island, who have gathered a pile of coconuts, which are to be divided the next day. During the night, one pirate arises, divides the pile into three equal parts, and finds one coconut left over, which he gives to the monkey. He then hides his share away from the pile. Later during the same night, each of the other two pirates, in turn, arises and repeats the performance of the first pirate. In the morning all three pirates arise, divide the pile into three equal shares and find one left over, which is given to the monkey. How many coconuts were in the original pile? Since the result is not unique, find all values from 1 to 1000 which satisfy the conditions.

APPENDIX II

HINTS TO PRACTICE PROBLEMS

All of the hints contained in this series have been developed in an attempt to help the beginning programmer.

1. Area of a square

   Data required.
   Use real Identifiers.
   Last data value should be 0.0.
   Output is a two column table showing the values of the side and the corresponding values of the area.

2. Area of a rectangle

   Data required.
   Use real Identifiers.
   Output is a three column table showing length, width, and area.
   Very similar to Problem 1.

3. Volume of a cylinder

   Data required.
   Use real Identifiers.
   Output is a three column table showing radius, height, and volume.

4. Squares of integers 1 to 25

   Use integer Identifiers.
   No data required.
   An important statement in the program is DO 10 I=1,25

5. Daily pay

   No data required.
   A possible statement is:

   ```
   DO 100 I=1,30
   ```

6. Fahrenheit to centigrade table

   No data required.
   Start program with DO statement.
   Conversion from integer to real necessary.
   The statement FA=I will accomplish this.

7. Finding the mean of 10 numbers

   Use real Identifiers.
   Ten data values required.
   AVE=SUM/10.0.

8. Compound interest

   Use real Identifiers.
   Data required.
   NC means N times C and the product represents the exponent.
   A possible READ statement is:

   ```
   7 READ,P,XI,XN,C
   ```

   A sample line of data is:

   ```
   100.0     .04     10.0     2.0
   ```

9. Sum and last term of A. P.

Use real Identifiers.
Data required.
A PRINT statement could be:

```
PRINT,A,D,XN,XLAST,SUM
```

A sample line of data is:

```
1.0    2.0    100.0
```

10. Sum and last term of G. P.

Data required.
Similar to Problem 9.

11. Solution of $AX^2+BX+C=0$

Quadratic equation.
Some knowledge of algebra required.
Data required.
Discriminant check necessary.
If (B^2-4AC) is negative, do not attempt a solution, instead, see if you can have the computer state "the roots are imaginary".
Use an H or Hollerith field.
The statement

```
READ,A,B,C
```

can be used to have the computer read three real numbers which will represent the numerical coefficients A, B, and C.

12. Solution of AX+BY=C and DX+EY=F

Simultaneous equations.
Data required.
Some knowledge of algebra necessary.
Determinants is one possible approach.
The READ statement could be:

```
READ,A,B,C,D,E,F
```

If you use determinants, be certain to direct the computer in case the denominator is zero.
A sample line of data could be:

```
5.    -10.    -20    8.    3.    25.
```

13. Finding the divisors of an integer

Data required.
One data value containing the chosen integer is sufficient.
Recall that when integer numbers are divided, truncation may occur; this is not true when real numbers are divided.
If B is a divisor of A then the quotient of A/B is the same in both integer and real.
If B is not a divisor of A then the quotient of A/B is not the same in integer and real.

14. Finding primes 1 to 100

No data required.
Assume 1 and 2 are prime and do not make them part of the test. The test is a divisibility check where each integer beyond 2 is divided by all integers from 2 to one half of the integer. If no divisors are found the integer is prime, and control passes to an output statement.
Whenever the computer finds that an integer has a divisor the testing terminates for that integer and the next integer is tested.
Two DO statements and two IF statements may be required.

```
DO 3 I=1,100                    4 goes to output
IF(I-2) 4,4,6                   6 continues program
```

15. Illegal cancellation

No data required.
Three nested DO statements will be required to check all possibilities.

16. Four digit numbers

Use integer Identifiers.
No data required.
Recall that when integer quantities are divided truncation may occur.
First statement can be:

```
DO 10 I=1000,9900
```

17. Loan problem

No data required.

The new balance is obtained each month by subtracting the amount paid on the principal from the old balance.

This program may be conveniently ended by checking to determine if the balance is less than $100.

```
Output:
1      1000.00       10.00      90.00
2       910.00        9.10      90.90
```

18. Mortgage problem

No data required.

Similar to Problem 17.

19. Addition table

The entire logic required to write this program is contained in the concept of the nested DO loop.
Only two DO statements required.
No data required.

20. Payroll problem

Data required.
This problem can be simplified by leaving out the employees' name.
If the program is to contain the employees' name, then a DIMENSION statement is necessary, and an A or Alphameric specification is also necessary in the formats.
With employees' name:

```
     READ,RATE,HOUR,PENR,BOND,TAXR,(N(J),J=1,7)
     1.50      40.      .08      18.75      .17      SMITH, JOHN M.
```

Without employees' name:

```
     READ,RATE,HOUR,PENR,BOND,TAXR
     1.50      40.      .08      18.75      .17
```

21. Grade point average

Data required.
Use real.
DIMENSION statement required.
Subscripted Identifier required.
Without name the statement

```
     READ,(A(I),I=1,8)
```

will read 8 real numbers from left to right for each student.

22. Perfect numbers

No data required.
Can be written using integer Identifiers only.
DIMENSION statement required.
Subscripted Identifier required.

Since the example indicates that 6 is the smallest perfect number, the statement following the DIMENSION statement can be,

```
    DO 10 I=6,100
```

The divisors of each integer (except itself) must be found and stored in an array.
These divisors must then be added, and their sum compared with the original integer.
If their sum is equal to the original integer, the number is perfect and control passes to an output statement which exhibits the divisors of the number and the number.
If the number is not perfect, control is returned to the first DO statement and the next integer is tested.
The entire array in which the divisors is stored must be set equal to zero each time a new integer is to be tested.
Assuming 10 locations are used, the two statements,

```
      DO 5 M=1,10
    5 ID(M)=0
```

will accomplish this.

23. Sorting problem

One of the more difficult programs to write.
Data required.
Subscripted variable.
The first two statements could be:

```
DIMENSION K(999)                      DIMENSION A(999)
READ(5,1) N, (K(I), I=1,N)    or    READ(5,1) N, (A(I), I=1,N)
```

The first data card should contain the number of 3 digit numbers to be sorted.
After the numbers are all read into the array, any two numbers can easily be compared (as to magnitude) by the use of the IF statement.
Their positions in the array can be exchanged by storing one of the values temporarily.
Two DO statements can be used.

24. Farmer problem

No data required.
Integer Identifiers required.
Three nested DO statements will check all the possible combinations
Two successive IF statements will check for 100 animals and $100 respectively.
Similar to problem 15.

25. Monkey problem

No data required.
Work in fixed integer mode exclusively.
An effective approach to this problem involves devising a divisibility check, since any number which satisfies the conditions of the problem must have the property that if one is subtracted from the number, the remainder must be divisible by three, and since 4 is the smallest possible number that has this property, we suggest,

```
DO 1 N=4, 1000, 3
```

as the first step of the program, and advise you to be looking for a series of four IF statements.

APPENDIX III

SAMPLE PROGRAMS THREE TO TEN

Sample programs one and two may be found in Chapter Six. Each of the following programs, except number ten, has been coded and run under WATFOR and FORTRAN IV. Number ten was coded and run only under FORTRAN IV.

SAMPLE PROGRAM THREE

PROBLEM: Write a program which will read in three numbers from a card, determine the largest of the three and print it out.

DATA: 1.1 3. -2.4

FLOW CHART:

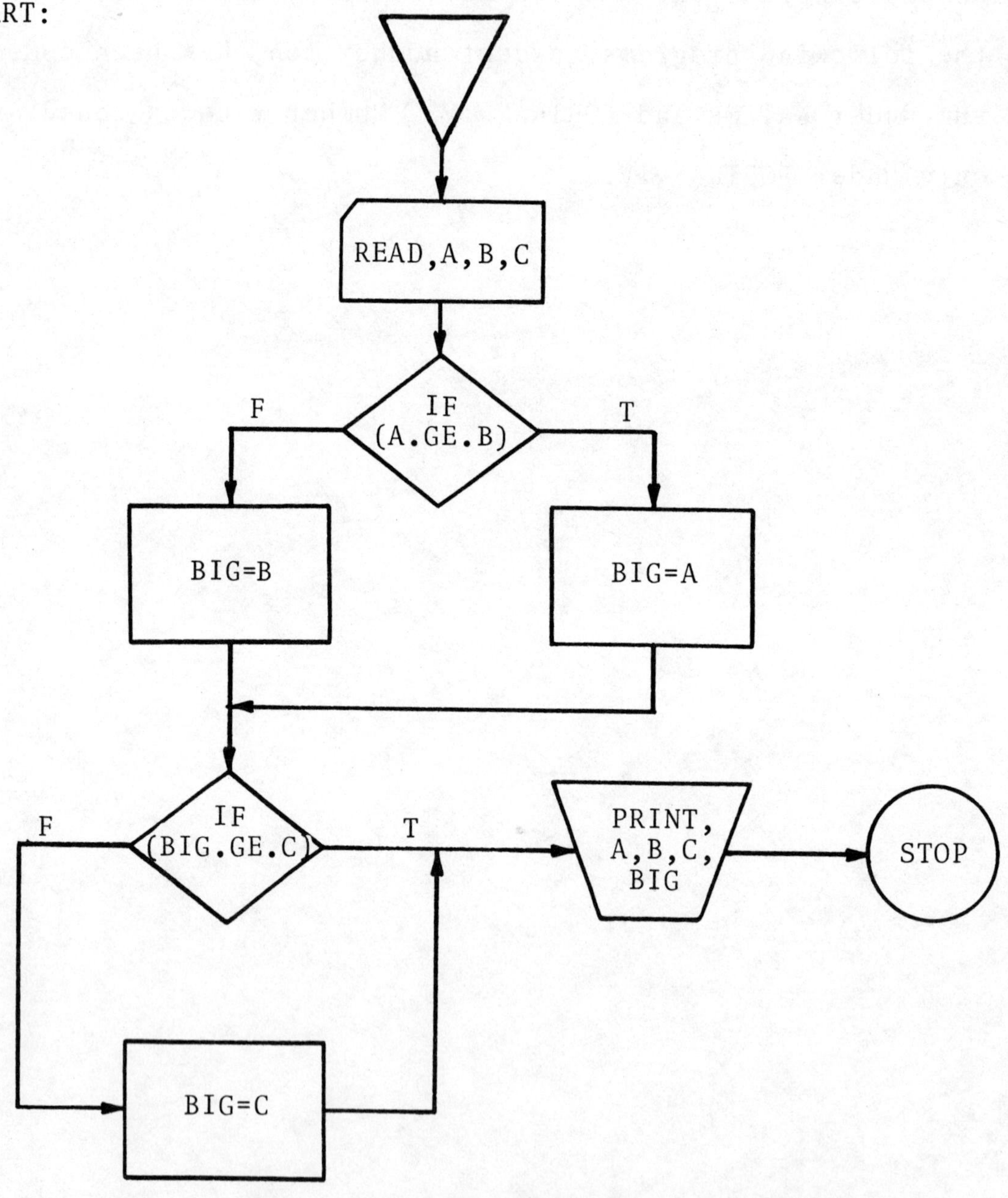

INPUT/OUTPUT (WATFOR):

```
C       SAMPLE PROGRAM THREE (WATFOR)
        READ, A,B,C
        IF (A.GE.B) GO TO 20
        BIG=B
        GO TO 10
   20   BIG=A
   10   IF (BIG.GE.C) GO TO 40
        BIG=C
   40   PRINT, A,B,C,BIG
        STOP
        END
```

```
 1.1        3.        -2.4
```

```
                1.100000                3.000000                -2.400000
                3.000000
```

INPUT/OUTPUT (FORTRAN IV):

```
C SAMPLE PROGRAM THREE (FORTRAN IV)
      READ(5,1) A,B,C
    1 FORMAT(3F10.4)
      IF(A.GE.B) GO TO 20
      BIG=B
      GO TO 10
   20 BIG=A
   10 IF(BIG.GE.C) GO TO 40
      BIG=C
   40 WRITE(6,28) A,B,C,BIG
   28 FORMAT(4F10.4)
      STOP
      END
```

```
   1.1000    3.0000   -2.4000    3.0000
```

SAMPLE PROGRAM FOUR

PROBLEM: Write a program to compute simple interest using the formula:

INTEREST = PRINCIPAL*RATE*TIME (TIME in years)

DATA:

Principal	Rate	Time
100.00	.04	10.0
5.00	.04	15.0
1000.00	.037	4.0
75.25	.0425	17.3
0.0	0.0	0.0

FLOW CHART:

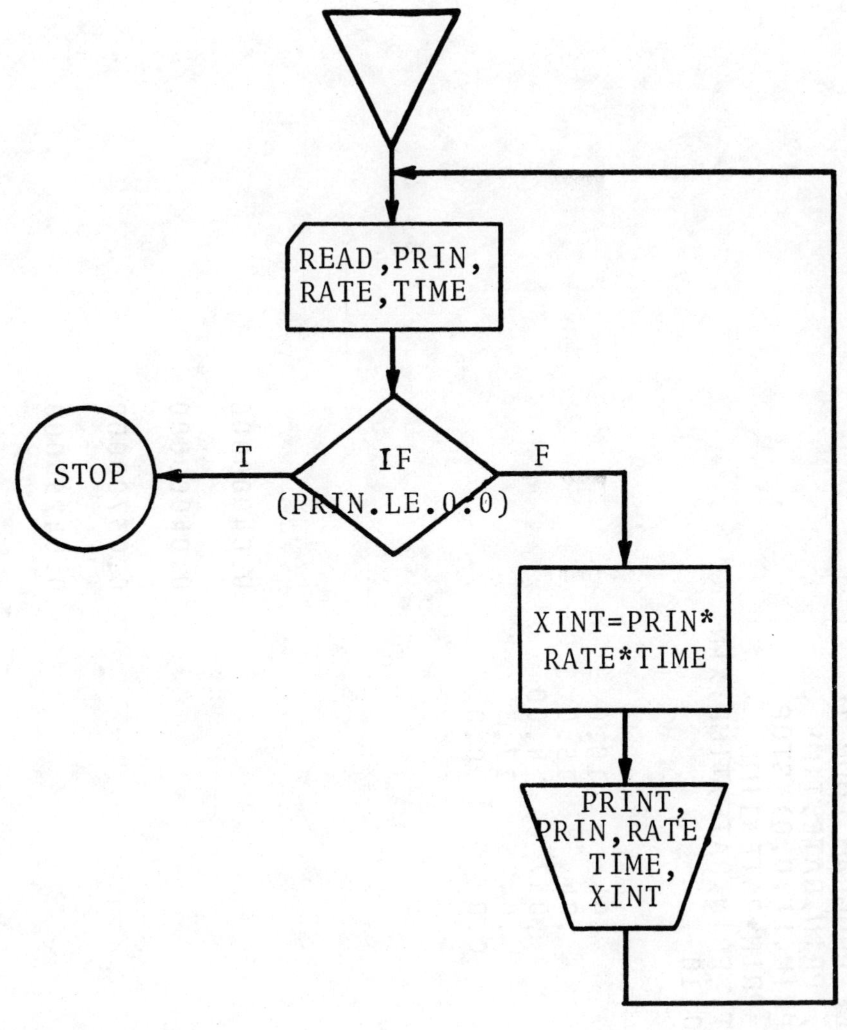

INPUT/OUTPUT (WATFOR):

```
C       SAMPLE PROGRAM FOUR (W[illegible]OR)
  10    READ, PRIN,RATE,TIME
        IF (PRIN.LE.0.0) STOP
        XINT=PRIN*RATE*TIME
        PRINT, PRIN,RATE,TIME,XINT
        GO TO 10
        END

  100.00        .04      10.0
    5.00        .04      15.0
 1000.00        .037      4.00
   75.25        .0425    17.3
    0.0        0.0        0.0
```

```
100.0000              0.04000000              10.00000
39.99998
5.000000              0.04000000              15.00000
2.999999
1000.000              0.03700000              4.000000
148.0000
75.25000              0.04250000              17.30000
55.32756
```

INPUT/OUTPUT (FORTRAN IV):

```
C SAMPLE PROGRAM FOUR (FORTRAN IV)
   10 READ(5,14) PRIN,RATE,TIME
   14 FORMAT(3F10.4)
      IF(PRIN.LE.0.0) STOP
      XINT=PRIN*RATE*TIME
      WRITE(6,28) PRIN,RATE,TIME,XINT
   28 FORMAT(F10.2,F10.4,2F10.2)
      GO TO 10
      END
```

```
  100.00     .0400     10.00     40.00
    5.00     .0400     15.00      3.00
 1000.00     .0370      4.00    148.00
   75.25      0425     17.30     55.33
```

SAMPLE PROGRAM FIVE

PROBLEM: Write a program to print a table for converting 1 to 12 inches to centimeters. (1 inch = 2.54 centimeters)

FLOW CHART:

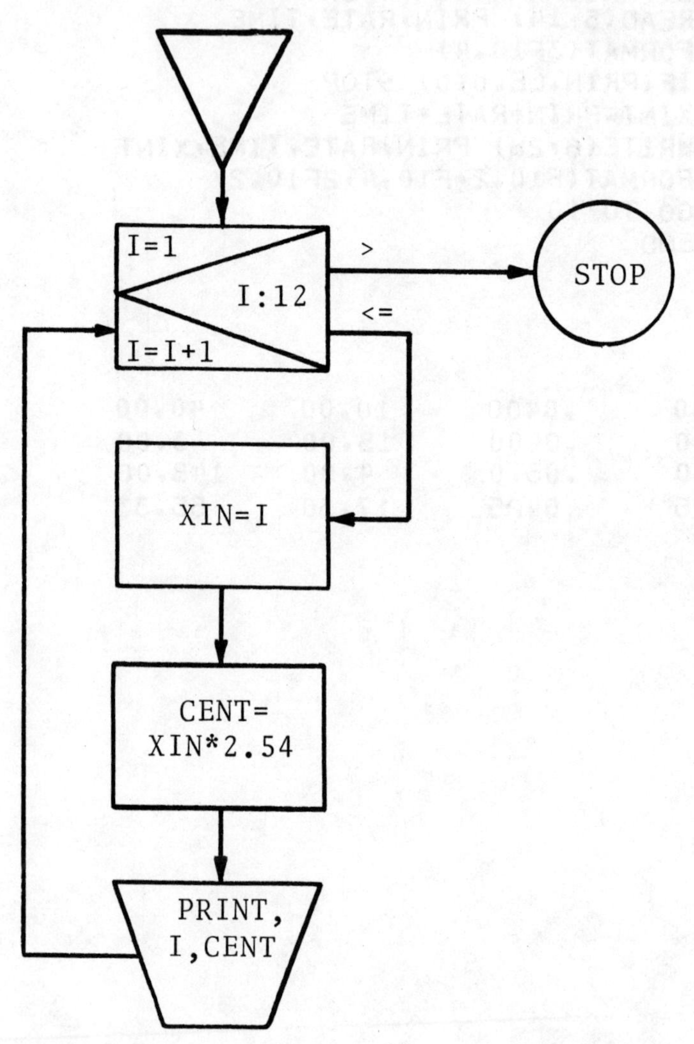

INPUT/OUTPUT (WATFOR):

```
C     SAMPLE PROGRAM FIVE (WATFOR)
      DO 100 I=1,12
      XIN=I
      CENT=XIN*2.54
      PRINT, I,CENT
  100 CONTINUE
      STOP
      END
```

```
   1                    2.540000
   2                    5.080000
   3                    7.620000
   4                    10.16000
   5                    12.70000
   6                    15.24000
   7                    17.78000
   8                    20.31999
   9                    22.85999
  10                    25.39999
  11                    27.93999
  12                    30.48000
```

INPUT/OUTPUT (FORTRAN IV):

```
C SAMPLE PROGRAM FIVE (FORTRAN IV)
      DO 100 I=1,12
      XIN=I
      CENT=XIN*2.54
      WRITE(6,34) I,CENT
   34 FORMAT(I10,F10.4)
  100 CONTINUE
      STOP
      END
```

```
         1    2.5400
         2    5.0800
         3    7.6200
         4   10.1600
         5   12.7000
         6   15.2400
         7   17.7800
         8   20.3200
         9   22.8600
        10   25.4000
        11   27.9400
        12   30.4800
```

SAMPLE PROGRAM SIX

PROBLEM: Write a program to print out a table of powers of 2 which are less than 1000.

FLOW CHART:

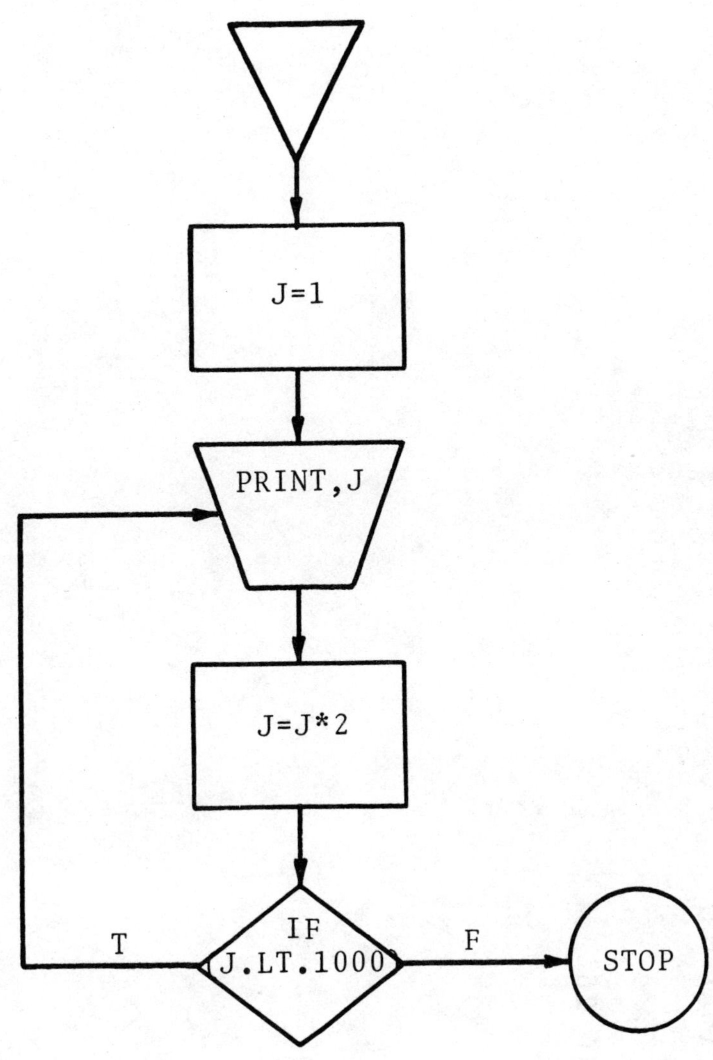

INPUT/OUTPUT (WATFOR):

```
C      SAMPLE PROGRAM SIX (WATFOR)
       J=1
   26  PRINT, J
       J=J*2
       IF (J.LT.1000) GO TO 26
       STOP
       END
```

```
     1
     2
     4
     8
    16
    32
    64
   128
   256
   512
```

INPUT/OUTPUT (FORTRAN IV):

```
C SAMPLE PROGRAM SIX (FORTRAN IV)
      J=1
   26 WRITE(6,43) J
   43 FORMAT(I10)
      J=J*2
      IF(J.LT.1000) GO TO 26
      STOP
      END
```

```
         1
         2
         4
         8
        16
        32
        64
       128
       256
       512
```

SAMPLE PROGRAM SEVEN

PROBLEM: Write a program to find the square root of any number, except zero. If the number is negative, print out its square root as an imaginary number, e.g. $\sqrt{-4} = 2I$.

DATA: 2.0, -3.0, 19.73, -15.96, 1234.5, -.0019, 0.0

FLOW CHART:

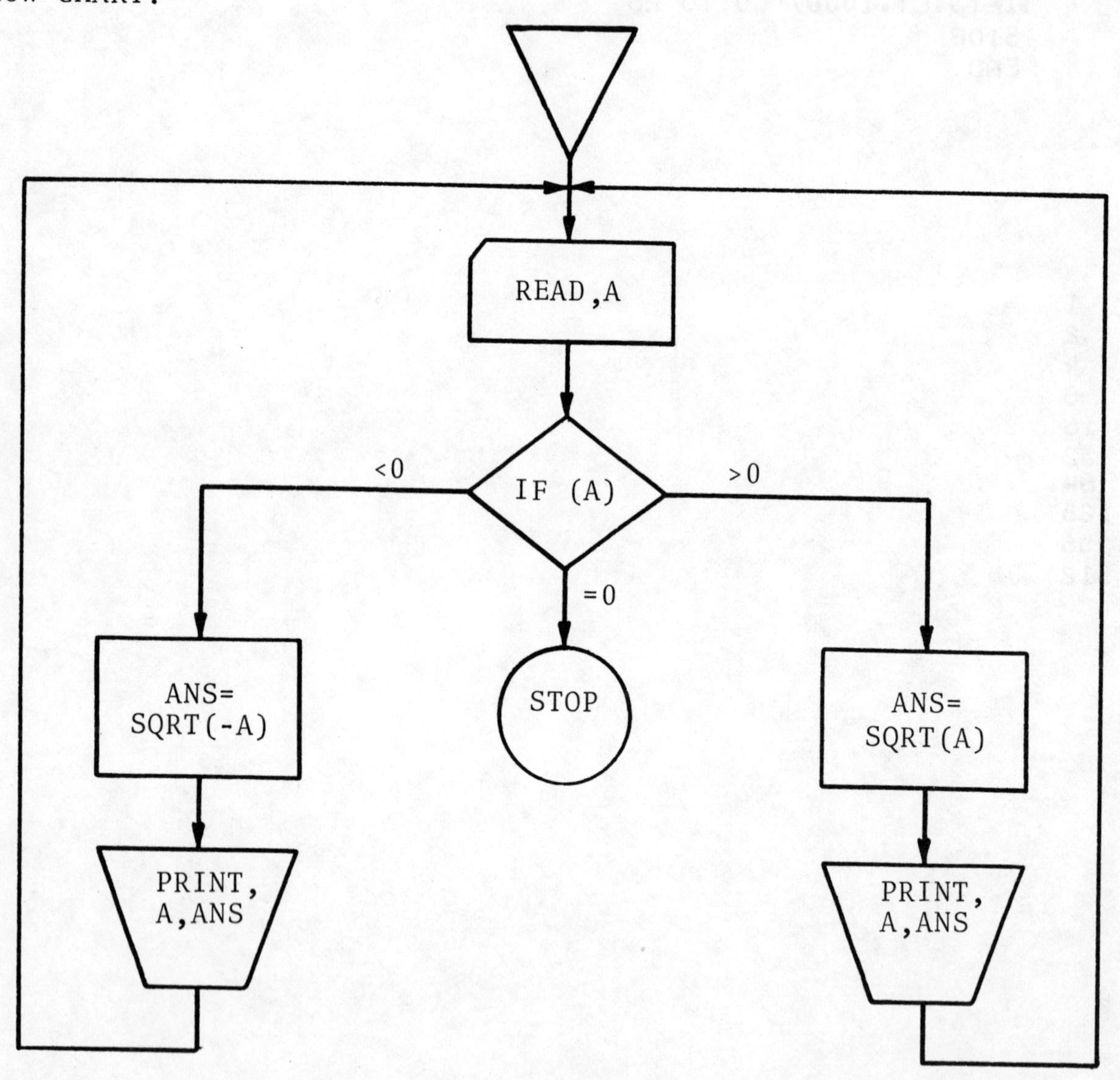

INPUT/OUTPUT (WATFOR):

```
C       SAMPLE PROGRAM SEVEN (WATFOR)
  12    READ, A
        IF (A) 14,26,93
  93    ANS=SQRT(A)
        PRINT, A,ANS
        GO TO 12
  14    ANS=SQRT(-A)
        PRINT, A,ANS,'I'
        GO TO 12
  26    STOP
        END
```

```
   25.0
  -49.0
    2.0
   -3.0
   19.73
  -15.96
 1234.5
   -.0019
    0.0
```

```
   25.00000                5.000000
  -49.00000                7.000000 I
   2.000000                1.414213
  -3.000000                1.732050 I
   19.73000                4.441846
  -15.96000                3.994996 I
   1234.500                35.13544
-0.001900000             0.04358899 I
```

INPUT/OUTPUT (FORTRAN IV):

```
C SAMPLE PROGRAM SEVEN (FORTRAN IV)
   12 READ(5,41) A
   41 FORMAT(F10.6)
      IF(A) 14,26,93
   93 ANS=SQRT(A)
      WRITE(6,46) A,ANS
   46 FORMAT(2F10.4)
      GO TO 12
   14 ANS=SQRT(-A)
      WRITE(6,47) A,ANS
   47 FORMAT(2F10.4,'I')
      GO TO 12
   26 STOP
      END
```

```
  25.0000    5.0000
 -49.0000    7.0000I
   2.0000    1.4142
  -3.0000    1.7321I
  19.7300    4.4418
 -15.9600    3.9950I
1234.5000   35.1355
   -.0019     .0436I
```

SAMPLE PROGRAM EIGHT

PROBLEM: Write a program to read ten numbers into an array, find the values of the largest and smallest numbers in the array, and print out these two numbers, along with the ten numbers in the array.

DATA:	.25	-173.65	0.0	3.1416	3.0
	-1.0	3.0	7.4	-3.78	11.

FLOW CHART:

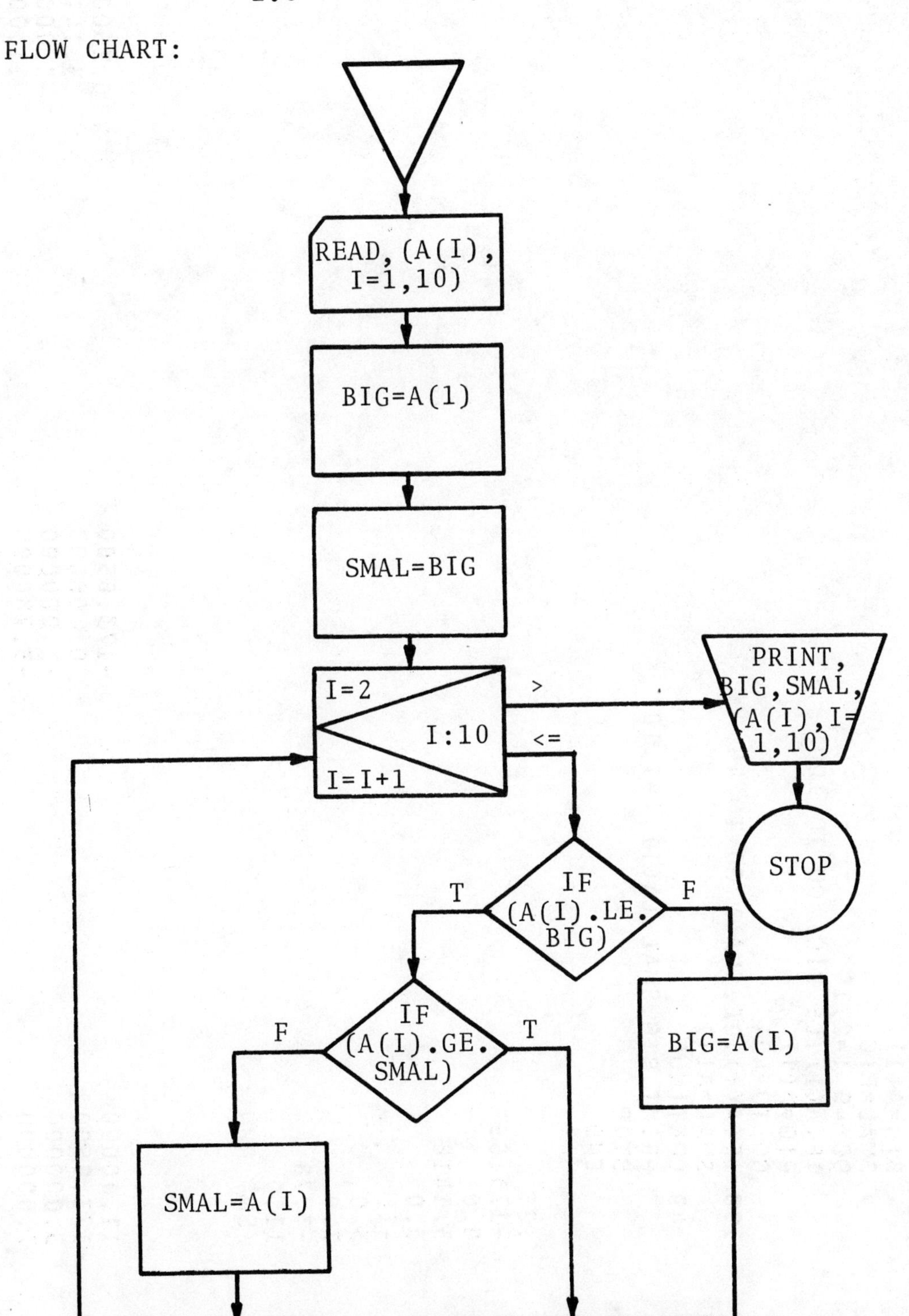

INPUT/OUTPUT (WATFOR):

```
C       SAMPLE PROGRAM EIGHT (WATFOR)
        DIMENSION A(10)
        READ,(A(I),I=1,10)
        BIG=A(1)
        SMAL=BIG
        DO 49 I=2,10
        IF(A(I).LE.BIG) GO TO 100
        BIG=A(I)
        GO TO 49
   100  IF(A(I).GE.SMAL) GO TO 49
        SMAL=A(I)
    49  CONTINUE
        PRINT,BIG,SMAL,(A(I),I=1,10)
        STOP
        END

   .25
   -173.65
   0.0
   3.1416
   3.0
   -1.
   3.0
   7.0
   -3.78
   11.0
   /END RUN

   11.00000        -173.6500       0.2500000
 -173.6500          0.3 00000      3.141600
   3.000000        -1.000000       3.000000
   7.000000        -3.780000       11.00000
```

INPUT/OUTPUT (FORTRAN IV):

```
C SAMPLE PROGRAM EIGHT (FORTRAN IV)
      DIMENSION A(10)
      READ(5,82) (A(I),I=1,10)
   82 FORMAT(5F10.4)
      BIG=A(1)
      SMAL=BIG
      DO 49 I=2,10
      IF(A(I).LE.BIG) GO TO 100
      BIG=A(I)
      GO TO 49
  100 IF(A(I).GE.SMAL) GO TO 49
      SMAL=A(I)
   49 CONTINUE
      WRITE(6,92) BIG,SMAL,(A(I),I=1,10)
   92 FORMAT(2F10.4,/,(5F10.4))
      STOP
      END
```

```
 11.0000 -173.6500
   .2500 -173.6500     .0000    3.1416    3.0000
 -1.0000    3.0000    7.4000   -3.7800   11.0000
```

SAMPLE PROGRAM NINE

PROBLEM: Write a program to print out a four by four multiplication table. That is, one times one through four, two times one through four, up to four times one through four.

FLOW CHART:

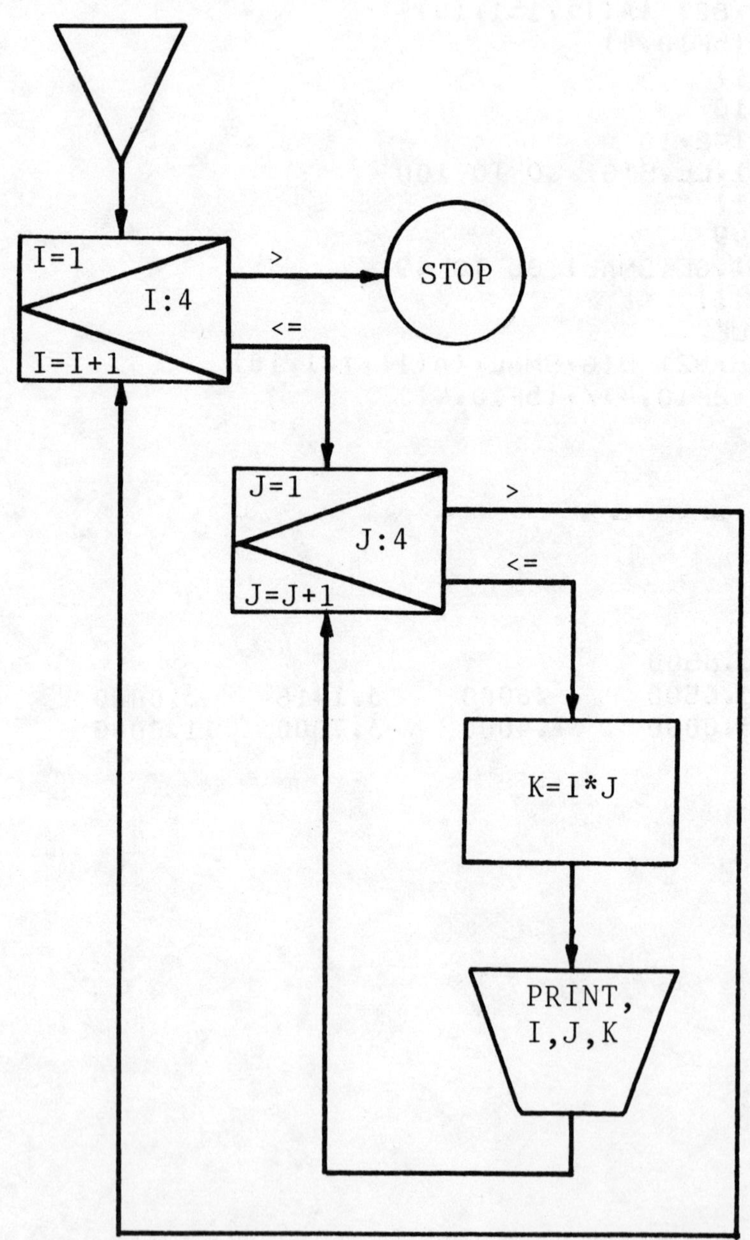

INPUT/OUTPUT (WATFOR):

```
C       SAMPLE PROGRAM NINE (WATFOR)
        DO 10 I=1,4
        DO 10 J=1,4
        K=I*J
        PRINT,I,'*',J,'=',K
   10   CONTINUE
        STOP
        END
```

```
 1 *            1 =            1
 1 *            2 =            2
 1 *            3 =            3
 1 *            4 =            4
 2 *            1 =            2
 2 *            2 =            4
 2 *            3 =            6
 2 *            4 =            8
 3 *            1 =            3
 3 *            2 =            6
 3 *            3 =            9
 3 *            4 =           12
 4 *            1 =            4
 4 *            2 =            8
 4 *            3 =           12
 4 *            4 =           16
```

INPUT/OUTPUT (FORTRAN IV):

```
C SAMPLE PROGRAM NINE (FORTRAN IV)
      DO 10 I=1,4
      DO 10 J=1,4
      K=I*J
      WRITE (6,1) I,J,K
    1 FORMAT (5X,I1,' * ',I1,' = ', I3)
   10 CONTINUE
      STOP
      END
```

```
1 * 1 =   1
1 * 2 =   2
1 * 3 =   3
1 * 4 =   4
2 * 1 =   2
2 * 2 =   4
2 * 3 =   6
2 * 4 =   8
3 * 1 =   3
3 * 2 =   6
3 * 3 =   9
3 * 4 =  12
4 * 1 =   4
4 * 2 =   8
4 * 3 =  12
4 * 4 =  16
```

SAMPLE PROGRAM TEN

PROBLEM: Write a program to compute the averages for a class of up to fifty students. The input data should consist of five scores and a name for each student. A negative value for the first score can be used to end the input. The output should show the name, average, and five scores of each student.

FLOW CHART:

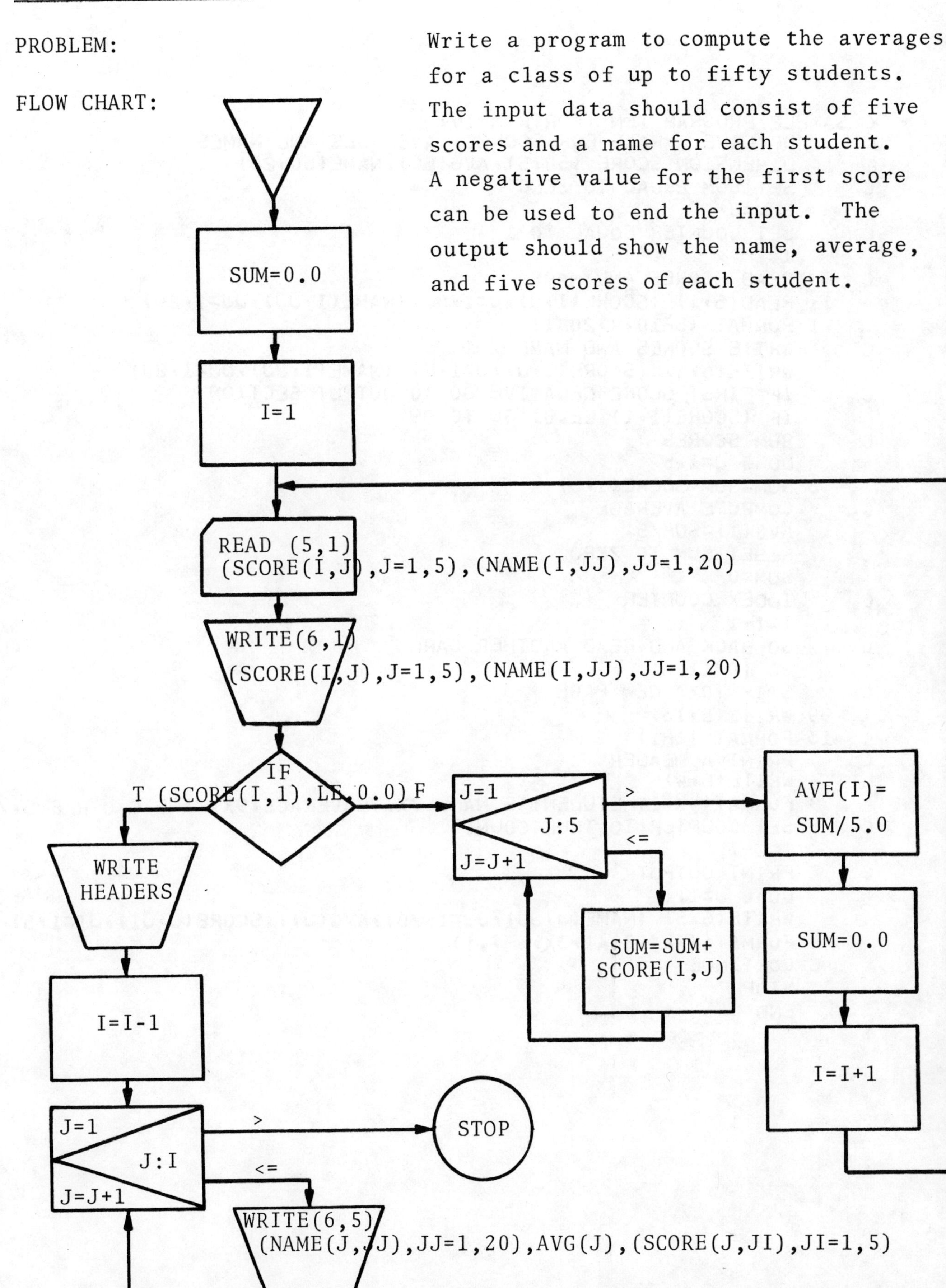

INPUT/OUTPUT (FORTRAN IV):

```
C SAMPLE PROGRAM TEN (FORTRAN IV)
C      DECLARE ARRAYS FOR SCORES, AVERAGES AND NAMES
       DIMENSION SCORE (50,5),AVG(50),NAME(50,20)
C      SET SUM EQUAL TO ZERO
       SUM=0
C      SET COUNTER EQUAL TO 1
       I=1
C      READ SCORES AND NAME
    11 READ(5,1) (SCORE(I,J),J=1,5),(NAME(I,JJ),JJ=1,20)
     1 FORMAT (5F10.4,20A1)
C      WRITE SCORES AND NAME
       WRITE(6,1) (SCORE(I,J),J=1,5),(NAME(I,JJ),JJ=1,20)
C      IF FIRST SCORE NEGATIVE GO TO OUTPUT SECTION
       IF (SCORE(I,1).LE.0) GO TO 99
C      SUM SCORES
       DO 3 J=1,5
     3 SUM=SUM+SCORE(I,J)
C      COMPUTE AVERAGE
       AVG(I)=SUM/5.
C      RESET SUM TO ZERO
       SUM=0
C      INDEX COUNTER
       I=I+1
C      GO BACK AND READ ANOTHER CARD
       GO TO 11
C      SKIP TO A NEW PAGE
    99 WRITE(6,13)
    13 FORMAT (1H1)
C      PRINT A HEADER
       WRITE(6,4)
     4 FORMAT(4X,14HSTUDENT'S NAME,7X,7HAVERAGE,9X,11HS C O R E S,/)
C      SET COUNTER TO TRUE COUNT
       I=I-1
C      PRINT OUTPUT
       DO 6 J=1,I
       WRITE(6,5) (NAME(J,JJ),JJ=1,20),AVG(J),(SCORE(J,JI),JI=1,5)
     5 FORMAT(/,2X,20A1,3X,6F7.1)
     6 CONTINUE
       STOP
       END
```

```
95.0000    87.0000    62.0000    74.0000    98.0000ADAMS, LYNN
90.0000   100.0000    95.0000   100.0000   100.0000BAUER, MARK
84.0000    86.0000    99.0000    86.0000    85.0000CARLSON, EDWARD
91.0000    70.0000    93.0000    91.0000    69.0000DAVIS, JANET
98.0000    99.0000    96.0000    96.0000    94.0000DIETZ, JOSEPH
72.0000    84.0000   100.0000    74.0000    91.0000FIELDMAN, MARYLIN
91.0000    77.0000   100.0000    89.0000   100.0000GOLDSTEIN, CHARLES
76.0000    66.0000    98.0000    87.0000    72.0000HOLMES, DENNETH
91.0000    74.0000    75.0000    70.0000    77.0000JOHMSON, LORETTA
92.0000    88.0000    90.0000    79.0000    70.0000JONES, NEIL
76.0000    91.0000    67.0000    94.0000    69.0000KING, PHILLIP
96.0000    99.0000    92.0000    74.0000    86.0000LYON, DARLENE
81.0000    86.0000    72.0000    99.0000    90.0000MILLER, CHARLES
97.0000    95.0000    87.0000    94.0000    98.0000MUSSMAN, CHARLES
81.0000    98.0000    74.0000    83.0000    78.0000NAKAMURA, KIM
92.0000    97.0000    94.0000    95.0000    91.0000NUTI, JOHN
96.0000    99.0000    99.0000    90.0000    97.0000OLSEN, RUTH
93.0000    85.0000    96.0000    89.0000    90.0000PERRY, JUNE
93.0000    90.0000    92.0000    91.0000    96.0000ROSEN, BARRY
92.0000    99.0000    87.0000    83.0000    91.0000RUSSELL, LAURI
62.0000    75.0000    84.0000    76.0000    64.0000SANDERS, DOUGLAS
91.0000    85.0000    96.0000    99.0000    82.0000SMITHFIELD, NANCY
95.0000    95.0000    91.0000    94.0000    83.0000TARRSON, HENRY
89.0000    80.0000    99.0000    96.0000    99.0000TASHMAN, IRA
80.0000    75.0000    83.0000    63.0000    64.0000WHITE, KATHLEEN
-1.0000      .0000      .0000      .0000      .0000LAST CARD
```

STUDENT'S NAME	AVERAGE	SCORES				
ADAMS, LYNN	83.2	95.0	87.0	62.0	74.0	98.0
BAUER, MARK	97.0	90.0	100.0	95.0	100.0	100.0
CARLSON, EDWARD	88.0	84.0	86.0	99.0	86.0	85.0
DAVIS, JANET	82.8	91.0	70.0	93.0	91.0	69.0
DIETZ, JOSEPH	96.6	98.0	99.0	96.0	96.0	94.0
FIELDMAN, MARYLIN	84.2	72.0	84.0	100.0	74.0	91.0
GOLDSTEIN, CHARLES	91.4	91.0	77.0	100.0	89.0	100.0
HOLMES, DENNETH	79.8	76.0	66.0	98.0	87.0	72.0
JOHMSON, LORETTA	77.4	91.0	74.0	75.0	70.0	77.0
JONES, NEIL	83.8	92.0	88.0	90.0	79.0	70.0
KING, PHILLIP	79.4	76.0	91.0	67.0	94.0	69.0
LYON, DARLENE	89.4	96.0	99.0	92.0	74.0	86.0
MILLER, CHARLES	85.6	81.0	86.0	72.0	99.0	90.0
MUSSMAN, CHARLES	94.2	97.0	95.0	87.0	94.0	98.0
NAKAMURA, KIM	82.8	81.0	98.0	74.0	83.0	78.0
NUTI, JOHN	93.8	92.0	97.0	94.0	95.0	91.0
OLSEN, RUTH	96.2	96.0	99.0	99.0	90.0	97.0
PERRY, JUNE	90.6	93.0	85.0	96.0	89.0	90.0
ROSEN, BARRY	92.4	93.0	90.0	92.0	91.0	96.0
RUSSELL, LAURI	90.4	92.0	99.0	87.0	83.0	91.0
SANDERS, DOUGLAS	72.2	62.0	75.0	84.0	76.0	64.0
SMITHFIELD, NANCY	90.6	91.0	85.0	96.0	99.0	82.0
TARRSON, HENRY	91.6	95.0	95.0	91.0	94.0	83.0
TASHMAN, IRA	92.6	89.0	80.0	99.0	96.0	99.0
WHITE, KATHLEEN	73.0	80.0	75.0	83.0	63.0	64.0

APPENDIX IV

SOLUTIONS TO PARTIAL PROGRAMS

Solution to PARTIAL PROGRAM ONE

DECK:

```
/END RUN
0.        0.
3.        5.
2.        5.
/DATA
      END
      GO TO 10
      PRINT, R,H,VOLUME
      VOLUME=3.14*R**2*H
      IF(R.EQ.0.0) STOP
   10 READ, R, H
C     PARTIAL PROGRAM ONE
/LOAD WATFOR
/JOB GO
/INPUT
```

ISC/PRYOR 5081-10

INPUT/OUTPUT:

```
/INPUT
/JOB GO
/LOAD WATFOR
C       PARTIAL PROGRAM ONE
   10   READ, R,H
        IF(R.EQ.0.0) STOP
        VOLUME=3.14*R**2*H
        PRINT, R,H,VOLUME
        GO TO 10
        END
/DATA
2.        5.
3.        5.
0.        0.
/END RUN
*IN PROGRESS

COMPILE =    0.23  SEC
                         2.000000                          5.000000                          62.80000
                         3.000000                          5.000000                          141.3000

EXEC =    0.02  SEC

*END

*GO
```

Solution to PARTIAL PROGRAM TWO

DECK:

```
/END RUN
      END
      STOP
   30 CONTINUE
      PRINT, CENT,FEET,YARDS
      CENT=FEET*12.0*2.54
      YARDS=FEET/3.
      FEET=J
      DO 30 J=1,13
C     PARTIAL PROGRAM TWO
/LOAD WATFOR
/JOB GO
/INPUT
```

ISC/PRYOR 5081-10

INPUT/OUTPUT:

```
/INPUT
/JOB.GO
/LOAD WATFOR
C      PARTIAL PROGRAM TWO
       DO 30 J=1,13
       FEET=J
       YARDS=FEET/3.
       CENT=FEET*12.0*2.54
       PRINT, CENT,FEET,YARDS
   30  CONTINUE
       STOP
       END
/END RUN
*IN PROGRESS

COMPILE =    0.26 SEC
                    30.48000            1.000000            0.3333333
                    60.95999            2.000000            0.6666666
                    91.43999            3.000000             1.000000
                    121.9200            4.000000             1.333333
                    152.4000            5.000000             1.666666
                    182.8800            6.000000             2.000000
                    213.3600            7.000000             2.333333
                    243.8400            8.000000             2.666666
                    274.3198            9.000000             3.000000
                    304.7998            10.00000             3.333333
                    335.2798            11.00000             3.666666
                    365.7598            12.00000             4.000000
                    396.2400            13.00000             4.333333

EXEC =    0.10 SEC

*END

*GO
```

Solution to PARTIAL PROGRAM THREE

DECK:

```
/END RUN
0.0
8.21
7.6
6.3
5.1
/DATA
      END
      GO TO 5
      PRINT, X, XSQ
      XSQ=X*X
      IF(X.EQ.0.0) STOP
    5 READ, X
C     PARTIAL PROGRAM THREE
/LOAD WATFOR
/JOB GO
/INPUT
```

```
00000000000000000000000000000000000000000000000000000000000000000000000000000000
11111111111111111111111111111111111111111111111111111111111111111111111111111111
22222222222222222222222222222222222222222222222222222222222222222222222222222222
33333333333333333333333333333333333333333333333333333333333333333333333333333333
44444444444444444444444444444444444444444444444444444444444444444444444444444444
55555555555555555555555555555555555555555555555555555555555555555555555555555555
66666666666666666666666666666666666666666666666666666666666666666666666666666666
77777777777777777777777777777777777777777777777777777777777777777777777777777777
88888888888888888888888888888888888888888888888888888888888888888888888888888888
99999999999999999999999999999999999999999999999999999999999999999999999999999999
ISC/PRYOR 5081-10
```

INPUT/OUTPUT:

```
/INPUT
/JOB GO
/LOAD WATFOR
C       PARTIAL PROGRAM THREE
      5 READ, X
        IF(X.EQ.0.0) STOP
        XSQ=X*X
        PRINT, X, XSQ
        GO TO 5
        END
/DATA
5.1
6.3
7.6
8.21
0.0
/END RUN
*IN PROGRESS

COMPILE =    0.25  SEC
                           5.100000                          26.00999
                           6.300000                          39.68999
                           7.600000                          57.75999
                           8.210000                          67.40410

EXEC =    0.02  SEC

*END

*GO
```

APPENDIX V

ANSWERS TO TESTS

Answers to CHAPTER TWO TEST

PART 1. True or False		PART 2.	
1)	T	1)	h
2)	T	2)	p
3)	T	3)	a
4)	F	4)	k
5)	T	5)	n
6)	F	6)	j
7)	F	7)	r
8)	T	8)	i
9)	T	9)	s
10)	T	10)	e
11)	F	11)	c
12)	T	12)	d
13)	T	13)	l
14)	F	14)	b
15)	T	15)	g
16)	T	16)	o
17)	T	17)	t
18)	F	18)	f
19)	F	19)	q
20)	T	20)	m
21)	T		
22)	T		
23)	T		
24)	T		
25)	F		
26)	F		
27)	F		
28)	T		
29)	T		
30)	F		

Answers to CHAPTER THREE TEST

PART 1.

a)

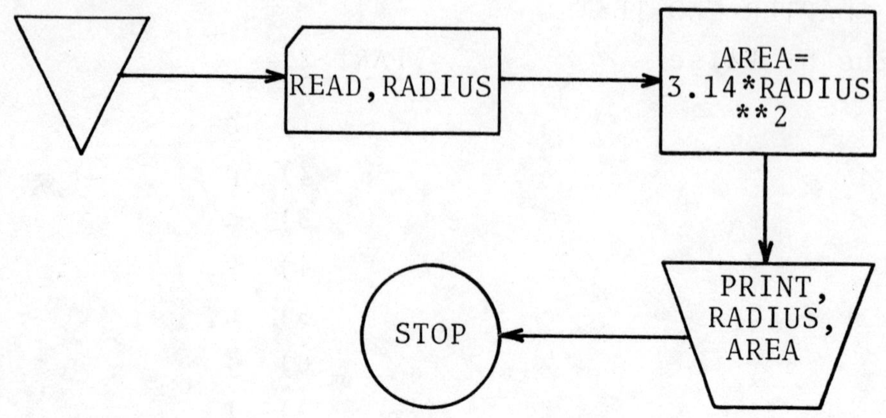

b)
```
READ,RADIUS
AREA=3.14*RADIUS**2
PRINT,RADIUS,AREA
STOP
END
```

PART 2.

1) c

2) a

3) d

4) b

PART 3.

a) READ,UP,DOWN

b) PRINT,A,B,C

c) A=2.4

d) correct

e) C=A+B

f) PRINT,HEIGHT,WIDTH

g) READ,AT,OUCH,BOG

Answers to CHAPTER FOUR TEST

PART 1.

1) g
2) h
3) e
4) j
5) d
6) b
7) a
8) c
9) f
10) i

PART 2.

a) PRINT,A,B,C
b) READ,RATE,COST,TIME
c) IF(A.EQ.B)STOP
d) READ,A,B,C
e) GO TO 1
f) IF(X.LT.Y)GO TO 4
g) PRINT,AREA,SIDE
h) GO TO 7
i) IF(A.EQ.B)STOP
j) A=3.14*R**2

PART 3.

1) T
2) F
3) F
4) T
5) F
6) F
7) F
8) T
9) T
10) F

PART 4.

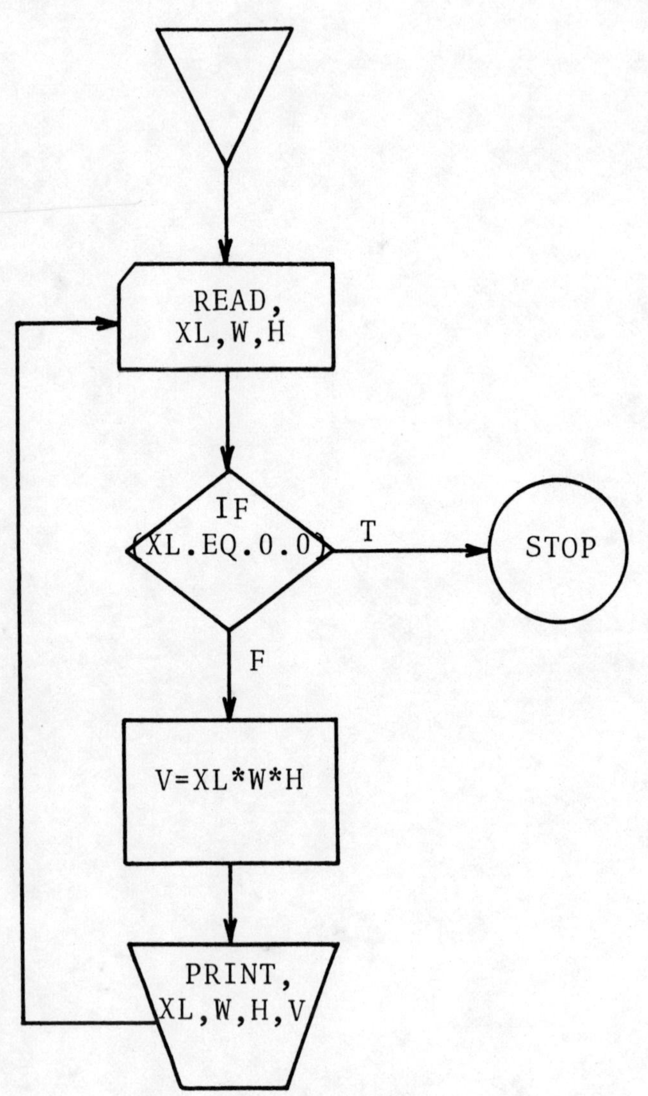


```
7 READ,XL,W,H
  IF(XL.EQ.0.0)STOP
  V=XL*W*H
  PRINT,XL,W,H,V
  GO TO 7
  END
```

Answers to CHAPTER FIVE TEST

PART 1.

a) 2

b) 50

c) 2

d) J>50

e) 25

f) 2

g) no

h) yes

i) DO 20 J=32,212,2

j) Only one line of output is printed.

PART 2.

```
    DO 100 J=1,20
    S=J
    AREA=S**2
    VOL=AREA*S
    PRINT,S,AREA,VOL
100 CONTINUE
    STOP
    END
```

PART 3.

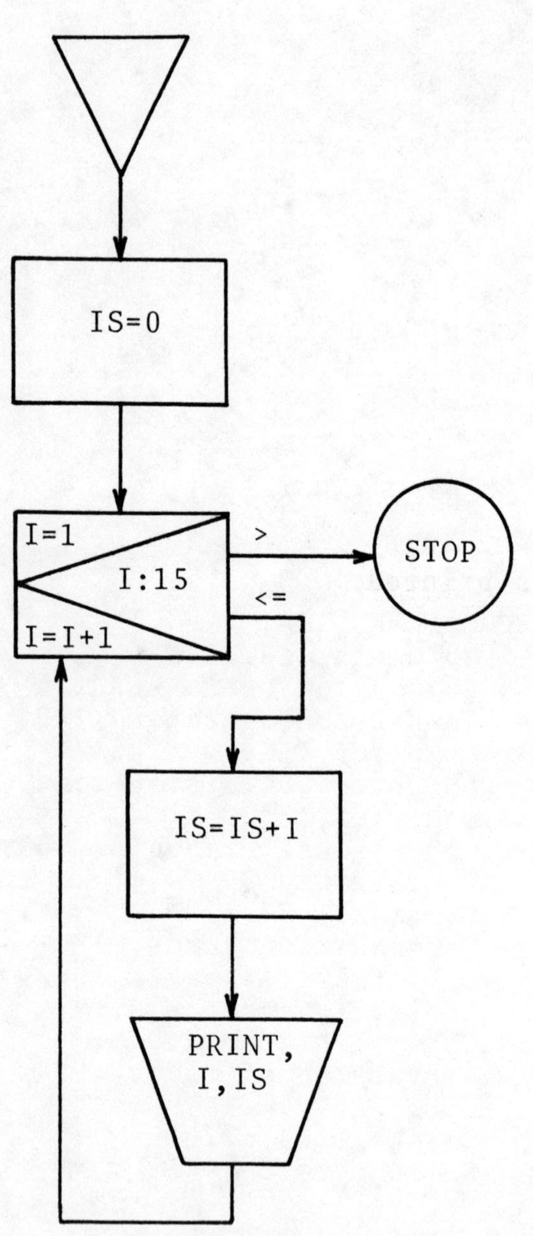


```
   IS=0
   DO 35 I=1,15
   IS=IS+I
   PRINT,I,IS
35 CONTINUE
   STOP
   END
```

INDEX

A

A format, 174
A specification, 174
ABS, 224, 226
Absolute value, 224, 226
Addition, 11, 13
ALOG, 226
ALOG10, 226
Alphabetic character, 11
Alphabetic strings, 169, 171
Alphameric data, 174
.AND., 209
Answers to Tests, 287
Arctangent, 224
Argument, 224
  in CALL statement, 233
  in FUNCTION subprogram, 231
  of built-in functions, 226
Arithmetic expression, 14
Arithmetic IF statement, 90, 204
Arithmetic operators, 11
Arithmetic statement function, 228
Array, 183
  doubly subscripted, 194
  Identifier, 183
  input, 185
  notation, 183
  operations, 187
  output, 188
  singly subscripted, 183
  size, 188
  subscript expression, 184
  sum of elements, 187
  triply subscripted, 197
Assigned GO TO statement, 203
Assignment statements, 14
  in sequence, 40
Assignment symbol, 11
ASSIGN statement, 203
ASTERISK,
  for exponentiation, 11, 23
  for multiplication, 11, 13
ATAN, 226

B

Base e logarithm, 226
Base 10 logarithm, 226
Binary representation, 5
Blank,
  character, 11
  field, 167
  in data, 127
  line, 178
  specification, 167
  use in spacing, 124
Branching, 83, 199
  conditional, 83, 200
  unconditional, 83, 199
Built-in functions, 224, 226

C

CALL statement, 233
Calling program, 234, 235
Carriage control, 178
Character code, 126
Character set, 11
Codes, 126
Coding, 124
Coding sheet, 125
Column, 194
Comments, 182
Common log operator, 226
Comparison operators, 207
Compiler, 179
Computed GO TO statement, 200
Computer, 3
Conditional branching, 83
Conditions, 99
Constant, 49
Continuation cards, 179
CONTINUE statement, 106
Control character, 178
Control statement, 84
Conversion of modes, 57
COS, 226
Cosine, 224, 226
Current value, 45

D

Data,
  card, 127
  declaration, 180
  generation, 109, 121
  list, 88, 127
  preparation, 155
  transmission, 67
  type, 180
DATA statement, 176
Deck assembly, 130

Declaration statements, 180
Degree, 224
Device number, 179
DIMENSION statement, 188
Division, 11, 13
DO statement, 103
  nested, 217
  summary, 117
Doubly subscripted array, 194
Dummy variables, 232

E

E exponent, 172
E format, 171
E specification, 171
Echoing, 89
Electronic computer, 3
END statement, 72
Equals,
  see assignment
  see .EQ.
.EQ., 91, 98
Equal to, 98
Error message, 90
EXP, 226
Exponent, 21
Exponential, 224, 226
Exponentiation, 11, 21
Expressions,
  as arguments, 234
  as subscript, 184
  evaluation of, 17

F

F format, 147, 163
F specification, 147, 163
Field, 147, 149
  width, 147, 153
  skip, 167
Fixed point mode,
  see Integer mode
Floating point mode,
  see Real mode
Flow chart, 6
Flow charting, 122
Flow chart symbols, 123
Flow diagram, 6
Format free,
  input, 145
  output, 145
Formats,
  A, 174
  E, 171
  F, 163
  H, 169
  I, 165
  X, 167
FORMAT specifications, 162
FORMAT statement, 145
  input, 153
  output, 147
FORTRAN, 6
Function,
  arguments, 231
  Arithmetic statement, 228
  built-in, 224, 226
  reference, 229
FUNCTION subprogram, 230

G

.GE., 98
GO TO statement, 87, 199
  assigned, 203
  computed, 200
  simple, 87, 199
  unconditional, 87, 199
Greater than, 98
Greater than or equal to, 98
Grouping characters, 12
.GT., 98

H

H format, 169
H specification, 169
Headings, 169
Hierarchy of operations, 27
Hints to Practice Problems, 247
Hollerith,
  card, 126
  field, 169
  string, 169

I

I format, 147, 165
I specification, 147, 165
IABS, 226

Identifier, 11, 14
  illegal, 15
  integer, 51
  legal, 15
  length, 15
  real, 51
  subscripted, 183
IF statement, 90
Illegal characters, 13
Incrementation, 111, 117
Index, 117
Index definition, 105
Indexing, 108
  increment, 117
Infinite loop, 90
Initialization, 111
Initial value, 117
Input, 67
  format, 153
Input FORMAT statement, 153
Integer mode, 49
INTEGER statement, 180
I/O, 67
Iteration,
  in DO statements, 104, 213
  in formats, 184

K

Keypunch, 126
Key word, 11

L

.LE., 98
Less than, 98
Less than or equal to, 98
Library function, 223
Line skip, 178
LIST,
  data, 88, 127
  see PRINT
    READ
    WRITE
Logarithm, 224
  common, 226
  natural, 226
Logical expression, 207
Logical IF statement, 90, 207
Logical operator, 209
Loop, 103
  nested, 217
Looping, 103, 217
Lower limit, 111
.LT., 98

M

Magnetic core, 4
Mathematical operators, 11
Matrix, 194
Memory, 3, 4
Message, 170
Mixed modes, 49
  exponentiation, 53
  expressions, 49
Mode, 49
  conversion of, 57
Multiple record format, 177
Multiplication, 11, 13

N

Natural logarithm,
.NE., 98
Nested DO loop, 217
Nesting DO loops,
  illegal, 218, 219
  legal, 218, 219
Normal exit, 214
Not equal to, 98
Numeric character, 11

O

One-dimensional array, 183
Operand, 99
Operations,
  array, 187
  order of, 27
  symbols for, 11
  see arithmetic operators
    comparison operators
    logical operators
    relational operators
.OR., 209
Ordering statements, 40, 46
Output, 67
  array, 188
  format, 147
Output FORMAT statement, 147

P

Parentheses, 32
  in order of operations, 37
  nested, 35
  required, 32, 35, 91, 99, 147, 178, 179, 183, 185, 189, 195, 200, 203, 204, 207, 224, 225, 229, 230, 233, 234
summary of rules, 37

Partial programs, 139, 140, 141
Powers of numbers, 21
Practice Problems, 239
Print positions, 147
PRINT statement, 68
PRINT with FORMAT, 146
Priority of operations, 27
Program assembly, 130

R

Radian, 224
Range of DO, 110
READ statement, 74, 179
READ with FORMAT, 146
Real mode, 49
REAL statement, 180
Relational IF,
  see logical IF
Relational operators, 98
Repetitive FORMAT specifications, 177
Replication factor, 150, 166
RETURN statement, 231
Right justified, 157
Row, 194

S

Sample Programs, 96, 132, 135, 253
SIN, 226
Sine, 224
Singly subscripted array, 183
Slash format, 177
Solutions to Partial Programs, 279
Spacing, 124
Special character, 11
Special exit, 214
SQRT, 226
Square root, 224, 226
Statement function, 228
Statement numbers, 85, 129
STOP statement, 72
Strings, 174
Subprogram, 223
SUBROUTINE, 232
Subscript, 183
Subscripted Identifier, 183
Subscript expression, 184
Subtraction, 11, 13

T

Test value, 111, 117
Three-dimensional array, 197
Transfer of control, 83, 87
Trigonometric functions, 224, 226
Truncation, 57
Two-dimensional array, 194
Type Declaration statement, 180, 181

U

Unconditional branching, 83
Unconditional GO TO statement, 87, 199
Upper limit, 111, 117

V

Variable,
  see Identifier
Variable format, 177, 178
Vector, 194

W

WATFIV, 179
WATFOR, 179
WRITE statement, 179

X

X format, 167
X specification, 167